VIETNAM WAR

FORENSIC & ANATOMICAL PATHOLOGY 1967-8
—ARMY CAPTAIN ANTON P. SOHN—
VETERINARIAN MEDICINE 1967-8
—ARMY CAPTAIN WARREN D. MYERS—
7TH SURGICAL HOSPITAL 1967-8
—ARMY CAPTAIN THOMAS W. BRADY—
MACV-SOG 1969-70
—NAVY LIEUTENANT RICHARD P. GANCHAN—

CAPTAIN ANTON P. SOHN MC U.S. ARMY
(HONORABLE DISCHARGE)

TotalRecall Publications, Inc.
1103 Middlecreek
Friendswood, Texas 77546
281-992-3131 281-482-5390 Fax
www.totalrecallpress.com

ISBN: 978-1-64883-150-8
UPC: 6-43977-41508-0

Library of Congress Control Number: 2022935129

FIRST EDITION
1   2   3   4   5   6   7   8   9   10

Colloform is trademarked

Vietnam War
is made possible by a grant from
Nevada History of Medicine Foundation, Inc.

This Book is Dedicated to

Vietnam Veterans:

Tom Brady MD, Jim Donadio MD, Al Rieser, Jr. MD

Bill Dawson MD, Joe Smalley MD, Bill Keeler MD

Dick Mason MD, Warren Myers VMD, Ed Katibah MD

Dick Ganchan MD, Bruce Farrell MD, Treat Cafferata MD

Mike Medawar MD, Charlie Johnson MD, Philip Weinstein MD

Al Garib MD, John Heumann MD, Jim Fulpert MD, Bill Illig MD

CONTENTS

+_+

Preface I

Introduction II

Vietnam War History IV

I: Forensic & Anatomical Path. 1967-8, Cpt. Anton P. Sohn 1

Goodbye Civilian Life... 1

Hello U.S. Army 1

Next Stop Fort Ord 10

Action Vietnam 12

Significant Forensic Pathology Events 12

Significant Anatomical Pathology Events 12

Significant Forensic and Anatomical Pathology Events are in Bold Print.................... 13

Second Honeymoon 39

Return to Action Vietnam 44

Saigon On Fire 53

Relaxing Hong Kong 56

Final Stop Saigon 59

Hello Civilian Life 63

II: Veterinarian Medicine 1967-8, Captain Warren D. Myers 71

III: 7th Surgical Hospital 1967-8, Captain Thomas W. Brady 78

IV: MACV-SOG 1969-70, Navy Lieutenant Richard P. Ganchan................ 85

Postscript: 94

Army 1958-9, 910 Med. Corpsman William P. Sohn............................ 94

Camp Bullis 94

Name Index... 96

I AM A "PROUD" U.S. Army VETERAN 98

PREFACE

+_+_+_+_+_+_+_+_+_+_+_+_+_+_+_+_+_+_+_

Vietnam Studies; Medical Support of the U.S. Army in Vietnam 1965-1970 1965-1970 by Major General Spurgeon Neel MD—Department of the Army, 1991 describes the 9th Medical Laboratory:

"The 9th Medical Laboratory from May to December 1966 was assigned to the 44th Medical Brigade. In December 1966, it moved to a newly constructed Vietnamese hotel 2 miles from the Lucky BOQ and approximately 2 miles from Tan Son Nhut AFB. The new facility was on a dirt road in an unprotected location. As a result of this unfavorable location, in June 1967, authorities decided to construct new facilities for the laboratory at Long Binh to be close to supply and personnel support units.

"The most essential workload at the lab was anatomic pathology and more importantly, forensic cases. Some of the workload was surgical pathology on biopsies submitted by volunteer surgical teams working with indigenous populations, such as the Seventh-Day Adventist Hospital. The processing of paraffin tissue sections and interpretation for U.S. Forces was centralized at the 9th Medical Laboratory."

INTRODUCTION

+_+

I vowed I would not write about my army career until I found the letter from President Lyndon B. Johnson starting with "Greetings". I have searched all my archives and could not locate the letter. Therefore, I am breaking my vow and recording my army career in the following pages. My military career started at the University of Cincinnati (UC), where I joined the U.S. Air Force Reserve Officers' Training Corps (ROTC). This was not a requirement at UC, but at the time it was a requirement at Indiana University (IU), where I finished my undergraduate studies. The UC program included training at Wright-Patterson Air Force Base in Ohio between my first and second year. When I transferred to IU for pre-med studies, my two years in ROTC at UC exempted me from ROTC at IU.

After graduating in 1961 from Indiana University School of Medicine, I interned at the San Francisco General Hospital when the war in Vietnam was heating up. My roommate at SFGH, Dr. Bruce Farrell, and I decided to join the Navy Fight School at Pensacola and become flight surgeons. I changed my mind, but Bruce went ahead and completed the training and entered the navy. Sad-to-say, Bruce was later killed in a helicopter accident in Vietnam.

My father died during my internship, and I returned to Indianapolis in 1962 to stay with my mother while I decided on a medical career. I did a general practice locum tenens in Dr. Victor Vollrath's office and decided to pursue a career in pathology. I met Arlene, got married, and moved to Tacoma, Washington in 1963 for a clinical, anatomical, and forensic pathology residency under Dr. Charles Larson, one of the world's foremost forensic pathologists. We were enjoying the Northwest when I got a letter in 1966 drafting me into the U.S. Army.

Before I got drafted, I told my Uncle William Fulton, who had served in the U.S. Hospital Corps in France during WWI (World War I) and as a dentist during WWII, that I could join the U.S. Public Health Service and avoid the draft. He sternly told me in no uncertain terms that <u>no one in our family had ever refused military service</u>.

When I was drafted, I had completed three years of the four-year residency required to be eligible for the American Board of Pathology examination. I was given one year credit for two years in the military and became board eligible after discharge. I passed the examination in 1968 and became certified in anatomical and clinical pathology. Because of my experience, I was certified in forensic pathology.

When I took the board examination in San Antonio, Texas in 1968, I walked on the sidewalk when a black man met me head-on. <u>I had to step aside to let him pass.</u> Life in the U.S. had changed since Martin Luther King, Jr. was killed earlier in 1968.

The following information is from handwritten notes and 454 pages of daily letters I wrote to my wife, my mother, relatives, and friends. Information from Thomas W. Brady, Warren D. Myers, and Richard P. Ganchan is from interviews.

IT IS MY HONOR TO SERVE IN
THE GREATEST MILITARY OF ALL-TIME!

VIETNAM WAR HISTORY

+_

Vietnam conjures many meanings. To the Vietnamese people, it means a war between communism and freedom. To France, it means a failed French colony. To America, it means a failed war that divided the country. To me, it means an interruption in my training to be a pathologist and a thrust into a leadership role.

The Vietnam War lasted from November 1955 to April 30, 1975, when the U.S. withdrew from Saigon. The war was fought between North Vietnam (supported by the Soviet Union and China) and South Vietnam (supported by the United States and anti-communist allies). The initial conflict was between the French colonial government and the Viet Minh, which lasted until 1954 when the French withdrew. The U.S. assumed financial and military support of the South Vietnamese state, resulting in guerrilla war between the Viet Cong (supported by North Vietnam) and South Vietnam (supported by the U.S.). By 1964 the U.S. had over 23,000 troops and advisors, and North Vietnam had 40,000 soldiers in the south.

A Gulf of Tonkin incident resulted when a U.S. destroyer was attacked by a North Vietnam attack-craft. President Lyndon B. Johnson ordered an increase of U.S. troops to 184,000. U.S. and South Vietnam forces relied on air superiority and overwhelming firepower to conduct search and destroy operations, involving ground forces, artillery, and air strikes.

In 1968 the Viet Cong (VC) launched "Tet Offensive" in the south and lost 50,000 men. By the end of the year, VC insurgents held almost no territory in South Vietnam, and their recruitment dropped by over 80% in 1969, signifying a drastic reduction in guerrilla operations and necessitating an increased use of regular soldiers from the north.

Following the Tet Offensive there was decreasing support among U.S. citizens for the war. U.S. forces had a period of morale collapse with disillusionment and desertion rates quadrupling from 1966 levels. Riots and anti-war protests broke out across America.

In 1969 Richard Nixon was elected U.S. President. Due to increasing opposition to the Vietnam War he began withdrawal of U.S. forces, placing increased reliance on South Vietnam forces.

The fall of Saigon resulted in the largest helicopter evacuation in history. It began on 29 April in an atmosphere of desperation, as hysterical crowds of Vietnamese vied for limited space to come to the U.S. It continued around the clock as North Vietnamese tanks breached defenses near Saigon. In the early morning hours of April 30, the last U.S. Marines evacuated the embassy by helicopter, as civilians swamped the perimeter and poured into the grounds to escape to the U.S. In an interesting sidelight, Vietnamese immigration resulted in Vietnamese restaurants springing up in cities across America.

On April 30, 1975, North Vietnam forces captured Saigon. This marked the end of the war. During the war 58,220 U.S. service members died and 1,626 were missing in action.

References:
1. Encyclopedia Britannica, March 5, 2008.
2. Kiernan, Ben: *Viet Nam: A History from Earliest Times to the Present,* Oxford University Press, February 2017.
3. Wikipedia.org/wiki/Vietnam_war.

I: FORENSIC & ANATOMICAL PATH. 1967-8, CPT. ANTON P. SOHN

GOODBYE CIVILIAN LIFE

After I received my draft notice, Tacoma General Hospital (TGH) lab personnel held a going-away party for me. The cake said "Good Luck! Volunteer Captain Sohn", ignoring the fact that I had no choice in the decision. I was instructed to report to Fort Sam Houston in San Antonio, Texas. Arlene was in labor with our first child, Anton Phillip, so I applied to U.S. Army headquarters for a one-week deferral, but the commanding officer, with "much" compassion, said, "No." Luckily Anton Phillip was born on April 28, allowing me to be present when he was born and drive nonstop to Fort Sam Houston to meet my induction deadline.

HELLO U.S. ARMY

Before I left Tacoma in 1966, I bought my first and last life insurance policy-$100,000 for two years. After driving from Tacoma to San Antonio, I checked in at base headquarters. The army was out of on-base rooms. The person in line behind me was Dr. Howard B. Corning. He and I were assigned a double room at the Wayhouse Inn.

A dress-blue-uniform was loaned to me by a pathologist friend, who was stationed at Fort Lewis, Tacoma. He said I would only have to wear the dress uniform once. He was right.

The first order of business at Fort Sam Houston was to assemble in a large amphitheater with approximately 500 drafted doctors. The officer-in-charge read off twenty names, including mine, who were to meet in front of the auditorium. I thought I have been selected for Vietnam, but because of my ROTC experience, I was appointed Platoon Leader of fifty doctors, Vietnam would come later.

Of interest, fifty-five years later in 2021, I reviewed the names of members in my platoon #7 and noticed that Dr. Thomas Scully, later dean of UNSOM and Robert Schrier, a classmate from high school were in my platoon. I knew that Dr. Schrier was at Fort Sam Houston but had forgotten he was in my platoon.

When Howard Corning was drafted, his grandfather gave him ten expensive cigars, which he shared with me. Each night after our military assignments we would smoke ½ of a cigar. Each day we met on the parade field, had roll call, received orders for the day, and marched to marshal music. While the other platoons were marching up and down the parade field bumping into each other to the amusement of career officers, I marched my platoon to the back of the parade field and gave the command, "Dismissed, Let's get the hell out of here". I wanted to show the army that I, not them, was in-charge. Boy, was I wrong! After our basic indoctrination at Fort Sam Houston, we were bused to Camp Bullis for one week of military combat-training.

At Camp Bullis we were involved in various combat exercises. We took training under fire by crawling across an enclosed area while live rounds were being fired above us. We also were taught to navigate by compass, during day and night. A Vietnamese village was constructed where we performed search-and-destroy activities. We also were taught the use of rifles and pistols. While in Texas I met high school friends, Harold Brown and Bill Ropp, who lived in Texas, for a day of relaxing at a Gulf of Mexico beach.

APS at TGH, goodbye civilian life

APS ready-for-war (Dress Blue uniform)

Harold Brown died in 2020.

Bill Ropp died in 2017.

Dr. Howard Corning graduated from Columbia College of Physicians and Surgeons in 1961. He was stationed in Japan. After military duty he had a successful medicine practice on the east coast. He died in 2005.

Dr. Bob Schrier graduated a year or two behind me from Indiana University SOM. He volunteered to serve three years in the army in Germany to avoid Vietnam and later, had a successful career at the University of Colorado School of Medicine. He died in 2021.

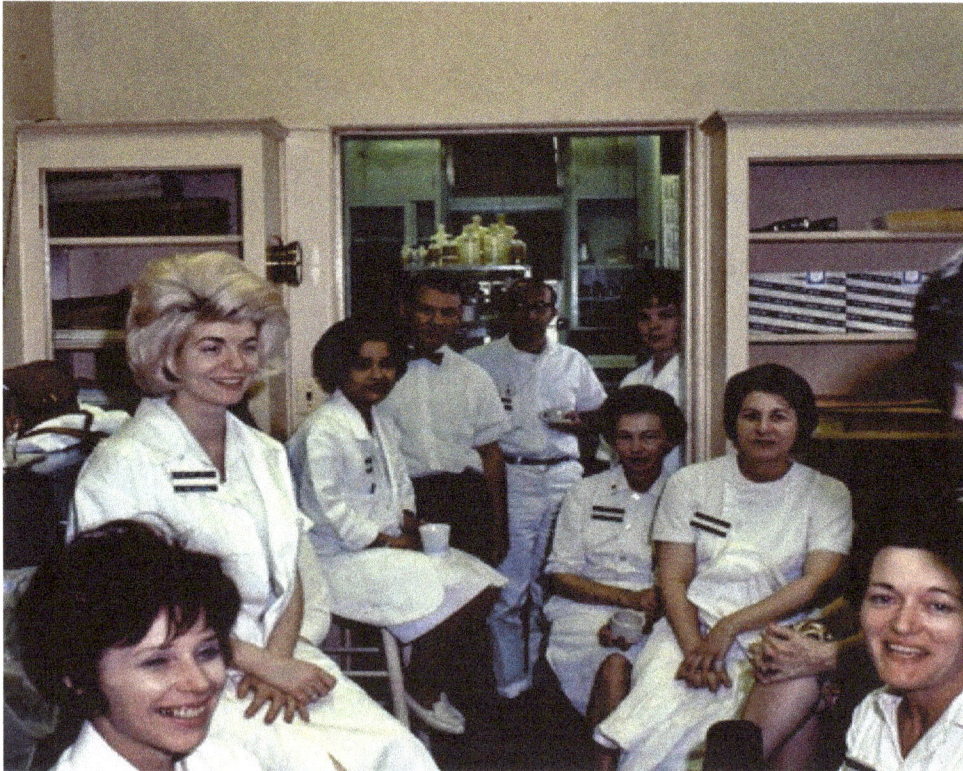

APS & TGH lab techs at my going-away party

APS, Wayhouse Inn, Houston, Texas

APS (white helmet) in constructed Vietnamese village at Camp Bullis

Going-away cake

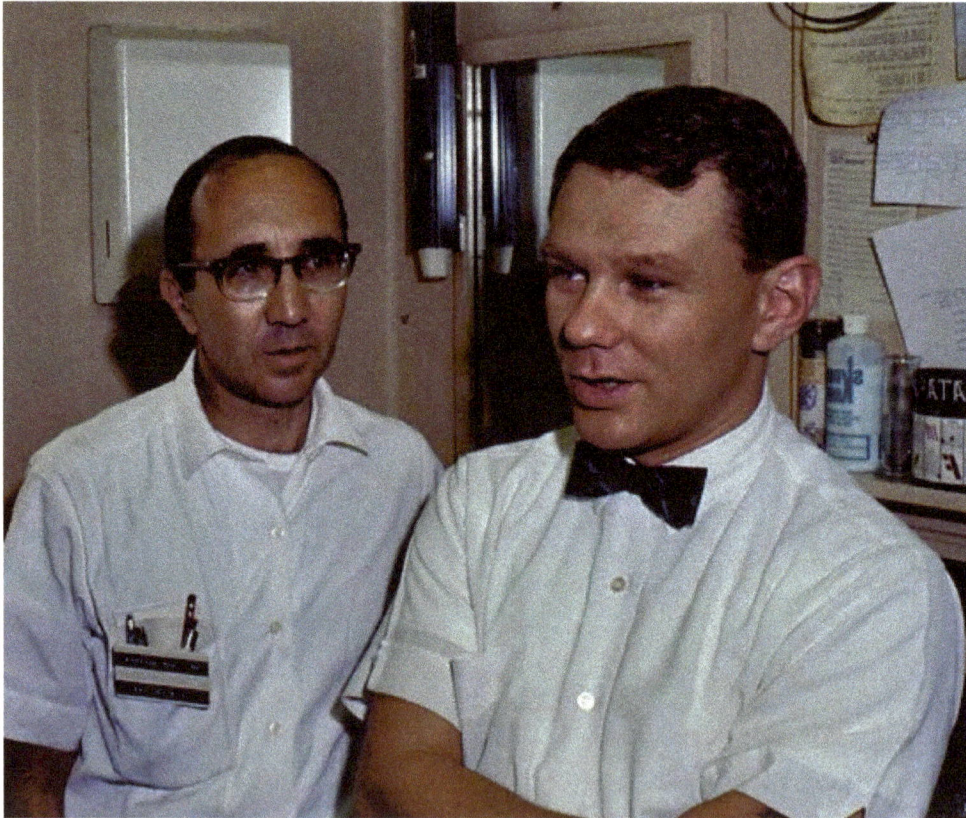

Tacoma General Hospital laboratory friend with APS

APS' Company A, 7th Platoon of 50 doctors at Fort Sam Houston

APS in Camp Bullis tent

APS and Bob Schrier writing letters in front of a soldier resting or dead

APS (white helmet) on the rifle range

APS with a foot on a "wounded" helicopter

H. Brown, B. Ropp, & APS, Gulf of Mexico

APS holding Phil at Fort Ord

NEXT STOP FORT ORD

From Camp Bullis I was assigned to Fort Ord, California. I drove to Fort Ord from Texas and Arlene drove from Tacoma with Phillip to meet me. At Fort Ord the handwriting was on the wall. I was one of three pathologists: Major George Knovick, Captain Al Rieser, and me. Since the workload only required one, <u>Vietnam here I come!</u> Later, Rieser was also sent to VN.

I was also required to take call in the emergency room. I only remember one patient. An officer came to the Emergency Room (ER) with a sprained wrist. I told him to wrap it with an Ace bandage and take aspirin. Because I didn't give him an Ace bandage and aspirin in the ER, he reported me to the colonel in charge of the hospital. <u>The colonel called me to his office and said a "few" words.</u> (After my military service I realized my error.) I remember one other event. From the ER, I was assigned to be the doctor at a softball game between retired officers. I was smoking a cigar when I saluted a retired general. I was quietly called aside and told "that was disrespectful". (I was learning military etiquette.)

More important, I reunited with Arlene and our new son, Anton Phillip. <u>Fort Ord was essentially a vacation.</u> We traveled extensively to the California coast, Yosemite, Death Valley, Napa wine country, and Grand Canyon. We also took classes at Monterey Community College, including French lessons.

In January we went to the Bing Crosby Golf Open on the Monterey Peninsula. We saw Arnie Palmer take a wedge shot that went three feet. The next shot went next to the hole. After one year at Fort Ord, I got orders for Vietnam. Before I left, Chief Pathologist George Knovick at Fort Ord made me a member of Loyal Order of the Pathfinder with a painting of me carrying a lantern.

Fort Ord was named in honor of Union Army Major General Edward O.C. Ord (1818-1883). The base was closed in 1994 and became a a National Monument, state university, and state park.
Captain Al Rieser, Jr. died November 4, 2020.

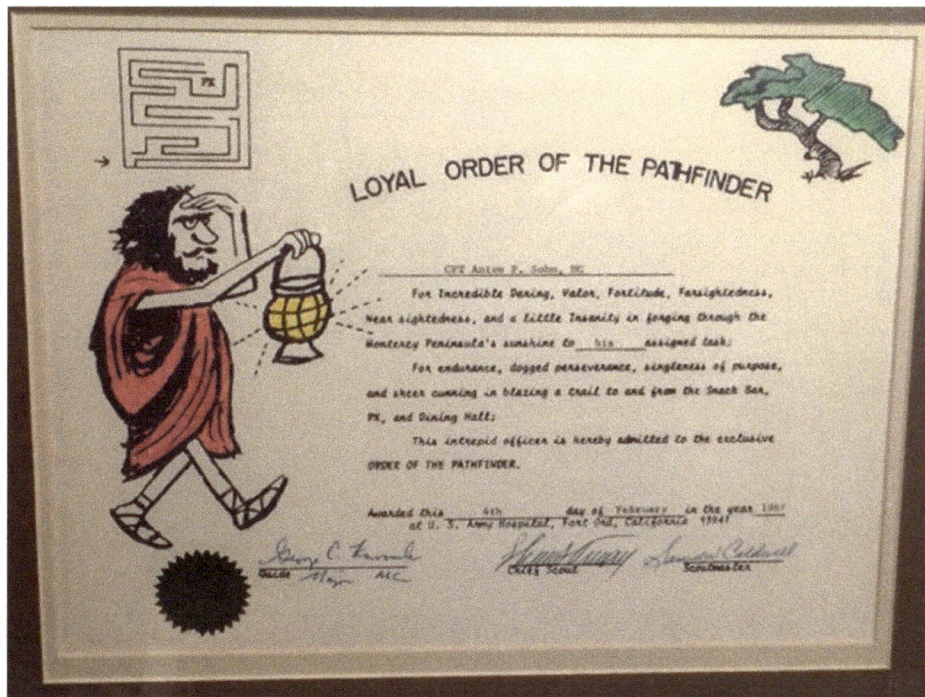

APS, Loyal Order of the Pathfinder

Our Fort Ord house at 402 Hays Circle

ACTION VIETNAM

When I received word that I was assigned to Vietnam I wrote a letter with my background experience in forensic pathology to the U.S. Army pathologist in charge of Vietnam. He replied that I would be stationed at the 9th Medical Laboratory. I sold my XKE Jaguar in Monterey and drove with Arlene and Phillip to Indianapolis in Arlene's car. We rented an apartment on the southside of Indianapolis for Arlene and Phillip before I flew to St. Louis and to Vietnam.

SIGNIFICANT FORENSIC PATHOLOGY EVENTS

1. Poison Brandy Death -- 15
2. Nonbleeding Shark Bite -- 16
3. GIs Rape and Kill Vietnamese Girl in the Boondocks ------------ 17
4. Blood on My Hands -- 19
5. Murder "From Heaven Above" -------------------------------------- 19
6. Murder/Suicide—Nurse/GI --------------------------------------- 23
7. Murder of a Black GI said to be an Accident ---------------------- 24
8. Murder?—Shot through the Anus --------------------------------- 44
9. Murder on a Dare --- 45
10. Hush-Hush Murder of a CIA Agent -------------------------------- 45
11. 9th Med Lab GI Fakes TB and Bleeding Ulcer -------------------- 46
12. GI Murders VN Girl in Vung Tau --------------------------------- 46
13. GI Struck by Lightning ------------------------------------- 47,52
14. Two Merchant Marines Kill VN Bar Girl ------------------------- 62
15. 9th Med Lab GI Fakes Gunshot Wound --------------------------- 48
16. Civilians Tried in Da Nang Military Court --------------------- 62

SIGNIFICANT ANATOMICAL PATHOLOGY EVENTS

1. One Autopsy Per Day --- 13
2. Reason for Military Autopsies ----------------------------------- 14
3. Betel Nut/Tobacco Cancers -------------------------------------- 14
4. Fourteen Autopsies in One Day ---------------------------------- 22
5. Tumors from Australian and Chinese Surgeons ----------------- 23
6. 111 Autopsies in 250 Days -------------------------------------46, 49
7. Surgical Pathology Case Load ----------------------------------- 59

SIGNIFICANT FORENSIC AND
ANATOMICAL PATHOLOGY EVENTS ARE IN BOLD PRINT

April 16, Sunday, 1967, Arlene's Uncle Corwin Alexander drove me from St. Louis to an Air Force Base one hour away in Illinois where I caught a flight to Denver. I remember the flight because I wasn't permitted to see the cockpit with its secret instruments. From Denver I took another military flight to San Francisco and a Greyhound bus to Travis Air Force Base. The next morning at 11:00 AM I took a 10-hour flight to Japan. From there I had a 4½-hour flight to Tan Son Nhut Air Force Base at Bien Hoa in Vietnam.

April 18, Tuesday, when I arrived, I was dead tired since I had only gotten 12 hours sleep in 2½ days since St. Louis. Upon stepping out of the plane at Tan Son Nhut Air Force Base, my first sensation was the smell of rotting vegetation. After I arrived at the terminal, I spent one night in a temporary holding tent before a jeep arrived from the 9th Medical Laboratory. Most soldiers spent 5 or 6 days in a holding tent. I was taken to a furnished apartment of a sailor, who was away. "Someone was looking out for me."

April 20, I was assigned a temporary room in the Virginia BOQ until there was room for me to move to the Lucky BOQ. The Virginia BOQ was in Cholon, the Chinese part of Saigon. It was five stories high without an elevator and had an enclosed courtyard. My room was on the fourth floor.

I talked to Jim Donadio, IU School of Medicine classmate, who was stationed about three miles from the 9th Med Lab at the 3rd Field Hospital.

I went to the 9th Med Lab. We had four pathologists at the lab. **We were doing one autopsy per day at Tan Son Nhut Air Force Base.** There was no sewer for the autopsy table, and the autopsy table drainage ran into an open trench. The morgue was easy to find. You just followed your nose.

I made $1,046 a month and put $985 per month from my salary into a savings account where I got 10% interest (it had a limit of $10,000 per year). My expenses per month were room $10, maid $5, laundry $5, and meals $30-45. The army paid me $65 per month for living expenses. Beer at the PX was $0.10 a can, a bottle of French wine was $5, and all items were inexpensive.

April 21, my schedule was to get up at 5:00 AM, shower, dress, walk to the Hong Kong BOQ, which was three blocks away, have breakfast, and then go in a military bus at 7:00 AM with about twenty lab personnel to the 9th Med Lab. At 5:00 PM we took the bus from the lab to the Hong Kong BOQ, had dinner, then watched a movie in an outdoor arena with about 100 people. The movies were old, repeats, and usually worth what they cost—$0.

April 22, the 9th Med Lab was a five-story converted hotel. My office was on the second floor. When I took call, I slept in my office on a cot with my pistol.

Two pathologists, Bill Illig and Dick Mason, were under my command, and the three of us did autopsies and surgical pathology for the U.S. Military in Vietnam. **We didn't do autopsies on military members killed in action. We did autopsies on individuals killed in accidents, murders, suicides, or dead from disease, which was about five per week. Helicopter accidents accounted for over 40% of the accidents. They flew at treetop levels and often lacked routine maintenance.**

Besides autopsies we did diagnostic pathology on surgical specimens from military instillations and the Seventh-day Adventist civilian hospital. **Most of their biopsies were from cancer of the mouth due to betel nut/tobacco chewing.**

The three of us alternated one week of surgical examinations and two weeks of autopsies. We had two office Vietnamese transcribers. An enlisted GI assisted with autopsies, and a GI photographer took photographs. The results were sent to the AFIP.

April 23, it seemed like we did a lot of autopsies on GIs who killed each other. Is it possible that they lost respect for life by the killing going-on around them? **Many of our autopsies were on crispy critters (burnt to a crisp) from helicopter accidents or green floaters (green marines) pulled from a river or a rice patty.** The autopsies from helicopter crashes were short. We did little more than take an x-ray.

April 24, Ed Katibah was a clinical pathologist at the 9th Med Lab. His primary responsibility was to install blood gas machines in labs around country. Several pathologists were stationed at field hospital labs around the country. Their primary responsibility was to examine blood smears for malaria. **I did an autopsy on a GI who died from ingesting methyl alcohol.** <u>He and a friend bought a bottle of French brandy on the street from a VN</u>. I saw the bottle. The bottom had been cut out and replaced. The contents had been replaced with a methyl alcohol mixture. **The GI's friend had permanent blindness**.

May 8, I did two autopsies. Both were natural deaths. One was a soldier who died in an epileptic seizure and the other soldier died from brain hemorrhage due to a ruptured aneurysm.

May 10, the day was slow, no autopsies or surgical specimens. After dinner at the Hong Kong BOQ, I rode in a jeep to the Virginia Hotel with a navy lieutenant, who said he was in an ambush on the river. My roommate had a friend who was shot in the chest, but it was a minor wound, and the shooter was killed.

May 15, each resident was supposed to stand guard at the Virginia BOQ every month or two, but I was excused because I was a doctor and a noncombatant. I swam or played handball every day, when possible, at the military events center. We were required to take an antimalaria pill every day.

May 20, I stopped at a VN art shop to look at a painting and found the artist had TB. I later took my stethoscope to examine him. His healthcare was not good, and his attending girl had a cough. I had to be on a constant watch-out for terrorists on the street. Last Friday, a Vietnamese soldier was shot by a VC couple on a motorbike a couple of blocks from our hotel. B-52s bombed a VC stronghold 12 miles from the lab, and the lab was really rocking. Also, not far from my hotel, a VC walked into a Catholic classroom where a GI was teaching English and shot him.

May 21, 9:40 PM, I went to the Hong Kong BOQ for a movie, *What's New Tiger Lilly* or something like that. It was a Woody Allen movie from Japan with English dubbed in.

Like most movies we got, it wasn't worth watching, but I watched the whole movie. This morning I stayed on the roof in the sun for about two hours, reading and listening to music (Jazz, Jimmy Rushin, and Count Basie) on a tape that Dr. David Huffman sent me. I saw a funeral procession go by the Virginia the other day (See page 33). It had one or two bands, depending on the wealth of the deceased. At the head was a roasted pig. The casket was in a cart that looked like a circus wagon.

An adult Caucasian male was found dead on a beach in Vung Tau. **After his arrival at the morgue, I immediately saw embalming incisions and bite marks that were large enough to be a shark bite. Obviously, an embalmed body does not taste good.** I was certain that he had been buried at-sea and washed ashore. Without doing an autopsy, I suggested he be taken further out to sea for burial. The embalming service at Tan Son Nhut AFB was managed by a French civilian, but it was not involved in the civilian cases.

We got a daily newspaper, *The Stars and Stripes*. It was 1/2 the size of a stateside newspaper and was folded like a book. It came to the lab free with one issue for three men, so I saw it about every two or three days. It had 1/2 page of pinups. Some called it the "Daily Sex Review". I sent my mother a watch for Mother's Day. A VN policeman was shot in front of the Virginia BOQ two days ago. The circumstance were hushed up and details won't be available for 4-6 weeks. Therefore, I took precautions.

May 22, 7:45 PM, I got three issues of the *Indianapolis Star* dated May 5, 8, and 9. They had better coverage of Vietnam than we received. We only got what Uncle Whiskers wants us to read. Everyone was a "short timer" or a "long timer". Obviously, I was a "long timer". Tomorrow is a Buddhist Holiday, some VN have the day off.

May 24, I became aware of the importance of sealing packages with perishables such as cookies and candy with wax paper. Some fellows in the lab received packages with worms because they were not sealed. Four days ago I mentioned a Saigon artist I had visited with TB. I guess you could say that I had a private practice. The artist's attending girl had a cough. Today I listened to her chest, and it was clear, so she just had an upper respiratory virus.

May 25, I sent a note to Fort Ord to find out when Dr. Al Rieser was coming. The 9th Med Lab assigns all in-country pathologists. Sunday of this week was my last Sunday in 14-15 weeks to be officer-of-the-day, as we had 14-15 officers in the lab. I wrote a letter to the American College of Pathologists to see about openings for pathologists. This proved to be unnecessary as my classmate, Dr. Ron Cudek, later found an opening in Reno for a pathologist.

May 27, after dinner I took a military bus to the Armed Forces' Library and got *To Kill a Mockingbird*, *The Moon and Six Pence*, *Jade*, *The Stone of Heaven*, and a book by Thomas Hardy.

There were two other fellows from Indiana at the lab, one was a career veterinarian, who graduated from Purdue. According to Warren Myers: "During the night, the major's name came to me. David Huxsoll, not sure of the spelling. I remember him telling me that he would take responsibility for all actions by the Veterinary Dept. at the 9th Med Lab since he was a lifer, and it would enhance his career. It would not make any difference to my career, even though I did all necropsies on over 100 dogs and all Rabies work. That was just one example of the military mind."

May 28, Sunday, 8:00 PM, I sat in my office reading about Hemmingway. I planned some time off for the following day because I completed my surgical specimen examination and didn't have much to-do. Our phone was out of order, and we were unable to get notices from the morgue.

Sunday, 8:00 PM, we knew that a body was coming to the morgue. **Several GIs raped and killed a VN girl out in the boondocks. We may only get bones to examine.** In this climate a body becomes a skeleton in no time.

May 30, we got an alert last night for an attack on the Virginia Hotel or Tan Son Nhut AF Base, but neither occurred. I stopped playing handball because it was too hard to get a court. Instead, I swam 1/4 miles per day. My pay was $955.03 per month.

June 4, I did most of my writing and reading lying on my bed because the chairs were cheap, small, and uncomfortable. Friday night IU classmate, Dr. John Heumann, called. He flew in a helicopter to town and stayed at the 3rd Field Hospital. The adjutant at his 12th Evac Hospital gave him fake orders and didn't enter them in the records. John was planning on going to Bangkok but couldn't get a seat on a plane. We went to dinner at a French restaurant. I had French onion soup, Burgundy snails, and duck with onions for $10.50. The soup was the most delicious I had ever eaten. John was stationed at Cu Chi, 15-20 miles outside Saigon. Cu Chi was an opening in the jungle with tents without running water or toilets. He said they got shelled about once a week and spent hours in an underground shelter.

June 7, I couldn't take a shower because the electricity was off. The electric pump that lifts the water from the ground to a reservoir on the roof was off. This was a regular occurrence.

I met Al Rieser's CO, who was setting up an autopsy and examine compound about three miles from us. They had 43 men, including three pathologists and two surgeons to dissect missile wounds.

June 9, while on the roof reading, there were about 20 large explosions in the Delta 20 miles from here. We saw the explosion; it took 20 seconds for the sound to reach us.

June 11, a fellow I knew at Fort Ord, whose name I can't recall, called. He arrived in May and was stationed up-country. We went to a floating Chinese restaurant in the Saigon River. It had been blown-up two or three years prior and 20-30 people were killed.

I presume they were subsequently paying off the VC. <u>When I got home, I realized a Korean soldier had moved in next door and was using my private toothbrush glass.</u>

June 12, I stopped at the PX bought frozen spareribs and corn on the cob to BBQ.

June 13, when I was going to breakfast from the Virginia BOQ, I was stopped at the entrance to Grenade Alley, (renamed Colt-45 Alley). The MPs asked if I was a doctor and showed me the body. I got there 45 minutes after an air force captain was killed. There were four jeeps, 12 MPs and 4 Comsots (VN police). The victim was covered with a rain parka. There were three 45 cal. casings near the body. **He had been shot in the back of the head and in the back. One shot had missed. They said he was shot by a girl on a motorbike driven by a VC. This was the third such killing in the past month.** I pronounced him dead and proceeded to the Hong Kong for breakfast. At breakfast I told my fellows from the 9th Med Lab about the killing. I said, if you don't believe me, look at the **blood on my hands**. I stopped going that way to the Hong Kong BOQ. Because of this and other similar incidents, we went from the BOQ to the lab in an armed truck. My fellow riders and I carried rifles. <u>If a motorcycle got close, we lowered our rifles. The motorcycle would quickly move away.</u>

We got three decomposed Vietnamese bodies with cards in their mouth that said, "From Heaven Above." A search and destroy mission entered a VN village where VC had been. Since they could be informants, the GIs got on the radio and asked their commander what to do. <u>He replied, "kill them".</u> Since there was a radio record of "noncombat" executions, the commander was in deep trouble.

June 19, we went to the roof of the Virginia and watched a very large battle in the Delta. There were massive explosions and helicopters firing 60 mm machine guns with tracers. It was so far away that we couldn't hear the sounds. My roommate took a shower and the water stopped when he was half done. I had to pour water on him from the drinking water. I took a tour of the *Germany Red Cross Hospital ship Hegoland* that was docked in Saigon. We did their pathology cases.

June 23, I saw two planes crash together last night over Saigon at 10:00 PM when I was on the roof. There was a large explosion, a secondary explosion and a mushroom cloud. A jet fighter crashed with a cargo plane. I saw the two parachutes of the two fighter pilots, who landed safely. Seven in the cargo plane died.

June 24, I got a nut cake from Arlene and a package from Mom, which was stamped June 20. Dr. Dave Huffman sent me a tape, so I had a heyday. I work tomorrow, Sunday, for a half day. This meant I would get Monday afternoon off.

June 26, we had seven pathologists at the lab. One was sent on the coast to Vung Tau, and another was sent to the 3rd Field Hospital. My mother sent some chocolate candy. I put it in the refrigerator and the maid ate it. I also got a letter from Aunt Amelia, Dad's sister.

June 28, the 9th Med Lab adopted an orphanage with 160 children, ages 3 to 9. I went over to check some of the children. <u>They had upper respiratory viruses and fungus disease of the scalp.</u> They had no refrigerators and cooked in an oven built out of rocks. Despite their condition, they were better off than most VN. The children needed summer clothes. My Korean neighbor took 30-minute showers and washed his clothes at the same time. A VN on a bike ran into my jeep. My driver didn't stop because the bike rider wasn't hurt. A GI from the lab had a similar accident, and the MP suggested he pay the rider about $45 US.

June 29, I saw Al Rieser and he said he was unhappy. He had been here one day. I was very kind and said everyone is unhappy here. He was living in an air-conditioned apartment with a pool on Tan Son Nhut AF Base.

July 3, I was appointed chief pathologist, not because of my brilliance, but because of my earlier date of rank. One of the pathologists, Jim Baker, at the 9th Med Lab was reassigned to Vung Tau, which was considered the safest place in VN, if that was possible. It was a former resort on the beach. <u>He was from Tennessee and was worried about getting killed (imagine that).</u> He said he was having trouble sleeping and eating.

July 4, no firecrackers going off here. I caught the maid making ice cubes for my refrigerator with tap water. I went to the roof and looked at the water in the tank. You wouldn't believe the stuff that was floating on the surface. <u>One of the pathologists in the lab got two weeks leave because he was close to "cracking up". Maybe I should do the same thing.</u>

July 9, I had a few $.10 beers with the pathologist who was going to Chu Chi with the 12th Evac. Hospital. I knew several fellows, who stayed in their rooms and drank alcohol every night. Some were afraid to walk on the streets due to recent couples on motorbikes, who do drive-by shootings. We were down to three pathologists in the lab. My maid spit-shined my shoes. They shone like glass, and I was the envy of my mates in the lab. I passed General Westmoreland and Robert McNamara (U.S. Sec. of Defense). They had 2 jeeps with MPs and 2 cars of newspaper reporters.

July 10, we had five autopsies, and I did three of them. All were aircraft accidents.

July 11, it rained hard most to the night. I was assigned to go to the gun range.

July 16, I went to the U.S. Forces Library and recorded Schubert's *Great Symphony* and *The Planets* by Gustav Holst. I went to a French Restaurant, *La Cave*, with friends. I had outstanding snails. Friday, a small in-stature Regular Army captain got on the bus. There were always 40 with about 10-15 standing. Sitting was first come, first served. The captain asked for everyone's attention and said, "As long as a captain is standing no privates should be sitting." Later a couple of majors and lieutenant colonels boarded and said nothing. Such is life.

July 19, we had a picnic at the special services beach. All the GIs brought their VN girlfriends (wives?) dressed in American clothes. The pathologist sent to the 12th Evac. Hospital said they live like pigs-in-a-pen. One GI was killed in the Hospital. John Heumann had left and was now at the 24th Evac. Hospital at Long Binh. We are going to get a VN girl who was raped and killed by GIs.

July 21, I am looking forward to getting out of the army in one year.

It seemed like most of the GIs were only concerned about their own hide. (I hope I am not complaining.)

July 24, I planned a trip to a provincial hospital to see if I could help.

July 25, since I was now the Chief Pathologist at the lab, the days went quickly as I had more paperwork to do. I planned to go to the library to record some music.

July 26, I moved to the Lucky BOQ to room with Bill Illig, who was also at the 9th Med Lab. The room was much nicer with a private bath and refrigerator. The room was on the fifth floor, but the elevators were not installed. I went to the library and recorded Handel's *Water Music*. I received a 5% discount on Arlene's ticket to Japan. She would make the reservations, and I would pay for the ticket.

July 27, when we moved into our room, our jeep was taken. I had asked the MP stationed at the front to watch. He decided to go inside and get a drink. He didn't tell his replacement to watch the jeep. A patrol car hauled my jeep away. I had to go to the office to get it back. <u>We were issued jungle boots (I still have them in 2021).</u>

July 28, I saw my new room. You wouldn't believe how poorly constructed it was, but it was much safer than the Virginia BOQ. The entire plumbing had to be replaced. They didn't put drains in the shower, so they had to knock a hole in the wall. <u>The shower was three feet in front of the toilet. Guess what that meant.</u> The refrigerators weren't delivered, so the Noncommissioned- Officer-in-Charge (NCOIC) said if we would buy one in the PX, he would reimburse us. This way he can resell it to the owner and make a profit. The U.S. government is paying the BOQ owner $6 per day for each room and there were about 100. We had 3 MPs and one Comsot at the front.

July 30, I got a letter from Dr. Ron Cudek. He said they were buying a house in Reno and there might be pathology job in Reno. My maid at the Virginia was better than the one at the Lucky. The NCOIC said they were 10 maids short, and we could ask her to move to the Lucky.

August 2, for several days I was taking a taxi to the lab. I thought it was safer than the bus because the bus always parked at the corner where there had been previous VC incidents.

August 4, we did 14 autopsies with three pathologists, which is a record. It took about two hours. They mostly involved an x-ray and a photograph since they were aircraft accidents. The result were crispy critters. Rieser got out of the hospital after one night. He had a reaction to an insect spray that he used to spray his room. I am studying for my pathology boards that I will take when I got back in the states.

August 6, <u>we did 29 autopsies last week. Twenty were from three separate aircraft accidents.</u> I got a letter from my cousin, Donald Howard, who has cerebral palsy. Donald graduated from high school with help from his mother (Aunt Mabel). His letter is worth copying to show the world that <u>those with CP can lead a happy and productive life.</u> He mentioned Home Place, the town where he lives, which was named by his mother.

August 11, I sent in a request for leave to go to Japan October 1. I had my first episode of diarrhea due to antimalaria pills.

August 15, Ed Katibah decided he wasn't going to take call with us, so we moved him out of the path office.

August 16, the lab's Commanding Officer (CO) was on leave, and since I was the longest serving officer, I was the acting CO. I had a driver and a car. The electricity in my BOQ was out again.

August 19, I did a murder-suicide. A signal corps captain shot and killed a nurse, who was his girlfriend, and then committed suicide. <u>They suspected the RN was pregnant. My lips are sealed.</u> The morgue was sealed off because of curiosity about the case. I got word that I will go to Nah Trang to testify on an autopsy I did on a sailor, who had been murdered.

August 20, I put a lamp in our closet to reduce mildew. A pair of my roommate's pants grew mold in one month. **We were seeing unbelievable tumors from Australian and Chinese surgical teams working in the provinces.** Bill Illig, who trained at the Mayo Clinic was very knowledgeable on diseases.

August 25, two pathologists came "out of the blue" to the lab, we had two with nothing to do.

August 27, I was notified I might have to go up-country and testify on an autopsy I did on a merchant marine, who was killed in a knife fight. I got another letter from Cousin Donald Howard. I took my first hot shower in four weeks. I went to the PX to get Tide, starch, bleach, and shoe polish for my maid. I did a case at the morgue of viral pneumonia. We had no way to determine the identity of the virus.

August 29, I treated an AF sergeant with antibiotics at the lab for a venereal disease. He didn't go to a clinic because it would be on his record. He snapped to attention and saluted me. He asked if there was anything he could do for me. He said he worked on the freight line and would send me a couple cases of steak (He did). We took 50 pounds of minced meat to the orphanage.

September 2, we got another career army pathologist. I didn't know where he would be stationed.

September 3, I had read 15 full-length novels during the past two months.

September 6, I got my passport for $10. I had GI problems for the past three days. I drew a plan of my 12 ft. x 18 ft. room at the Lucky. We had four pathologists in the lab. Two pathologists did autopsies and two did surgicals. One was scheduled to leave next week.

September 9, I read in the Amer. Med. Assoc.(AMA) paper that 2,200 doctors were getting drafted this summer. For sure some would spend time in Vietnam. **I did an autopsy on a black GI, who was alleged to have fallen down a flight of stairs. The autopsy showed that he was murdered, beaten-to-death.** There were multiple injuries only on the left side of his head, which meant he was hit multiple times with a blunt instrument.

The injuries were inconsistent with an accidental fall. I signed it out as a homicide and dispensed an MP to the base where he was killed. He said the blood was cleaned up where the GI was found. I never heard back. I've done my part. Someone knew who the killer was.

September 10, Sunday, I studied most of the day for my pathology boards. We had two feet of water standing in the lab parking lot. The monsoon had been here for three months.

September 11, our water supply to the room was out. My bedside lamp was made of beer cans.

September 24, I went swimming about three times a week. I was getting lots of cookies, nuts, and candy from relatives. <u>I gave some to GIs in the lab. Many don't get anything from family.</u>

September 25, we got another pathologist, who was sent to an out-country laboratory.

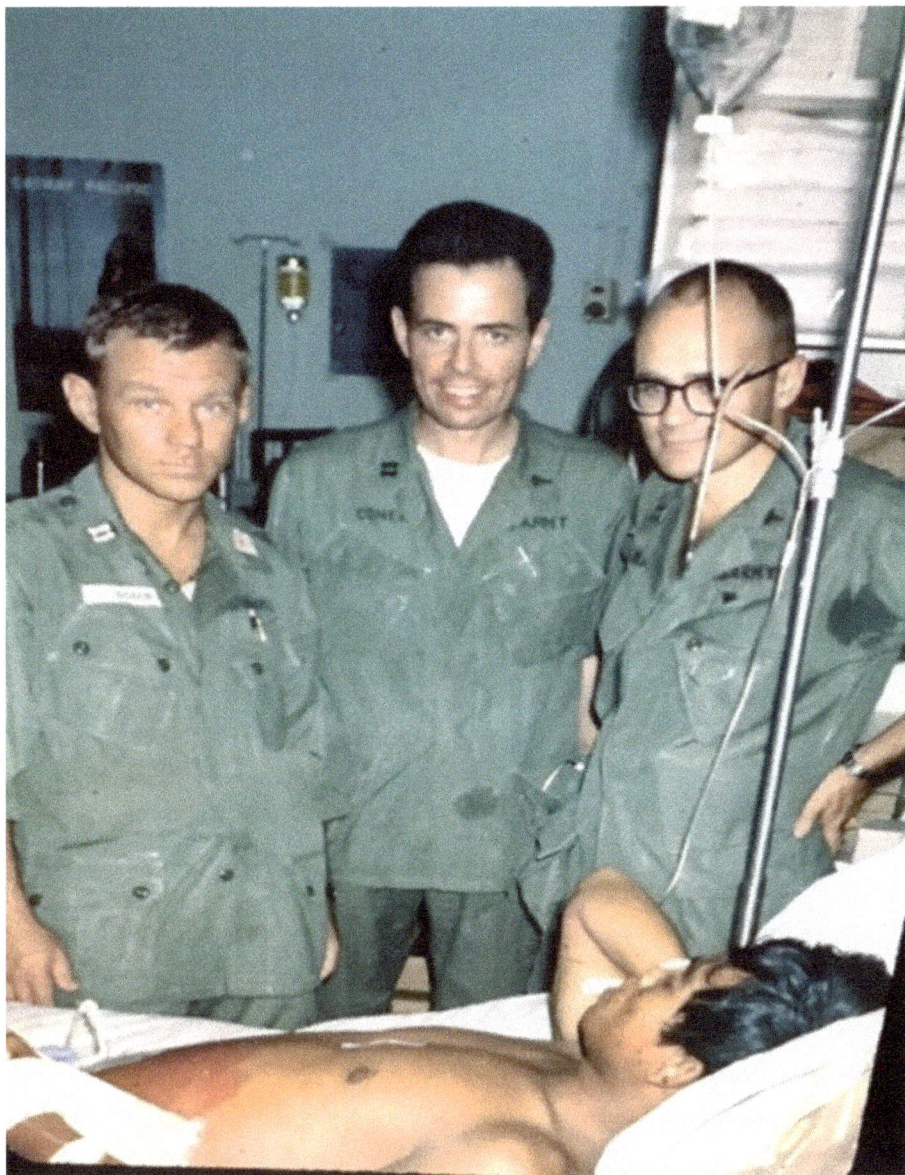

APS, Dave Cohen, & Dick Mason, 3rd Field Hosp.

Virginia BOQ

Tan Son Nhut Air Force Base when I arrived, 1967

APS, Lucky BOQ

Saigon street scene

9th Med Lab. My office is above the vehicle with the star

Typical homes on Saigon waterfront

A happy Vietnamese child with Batman

First Sergeant's pet hawk

APS gingerly relaxing on my office balcony ledge

VN truck in mud in front of 9th Med Lab

Our "battle-alert" VN driver

APS at the gun range

APS practicing defense with rifle

VN funeral procession in front of Virginia BOQ

Saigon street scene

Vietnamese hovels behind the 9th Med Lab

APS and German Red Cross Hospital Ship Hegoland, Saigon River

Special Services Saigon River Beach Facility

Drs. C. Johnson & APS at a Virginia BOQ barbecue

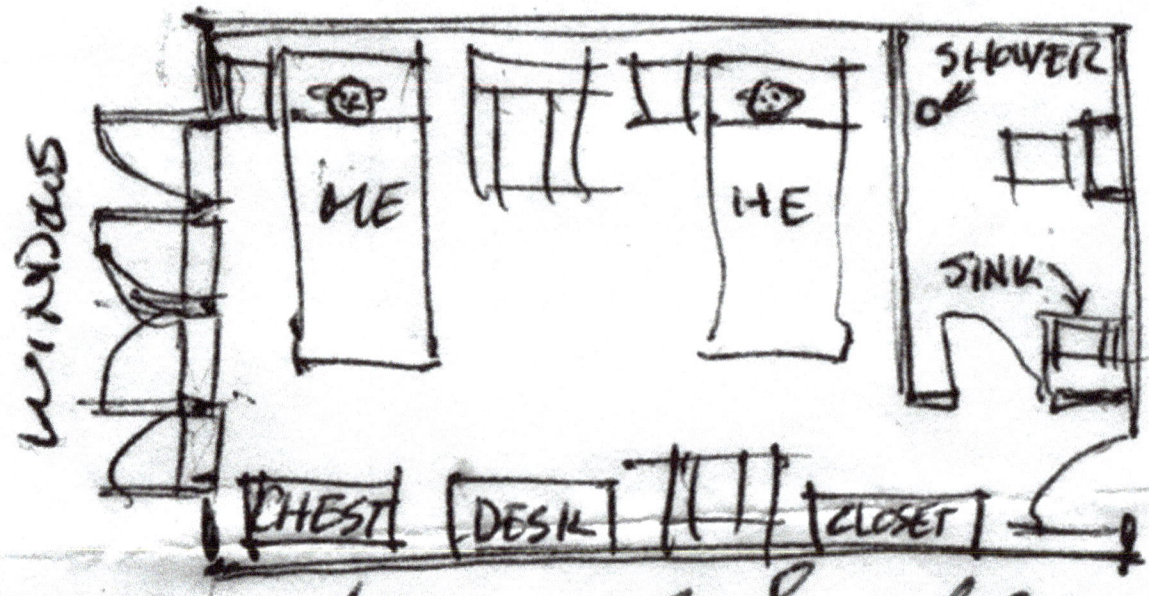

My 12 ft. x 18 ft. room in the Lucky BOQ

Special Services Library Entrance

French Cemetery, Saigon

Dear Andy;

I have been thinking about you for several days, and I haved been entending to write,
but like so many things I should do, I just keep putting it off. So guess this is
a good time to get started. Well the weather is just beautiful today here in Indiana
and Home Place. I just came in from a ride on my bicycle and it was just wonderful
out. I rode up Cornell (a street east of us) to 111th street and accross 111th
to College Ave and on back down College back home. Then sometimes I stop in and have
as chat with the boys at the corner barber shop at 106th & College. Oh-by the way
I have 835 miles registered on my spedometer and incidently I just had my bicycle
two years yesterday. I don't remember whether you have saw it or not, but maybe you
have heard the folks talk about it. It is a Schwinn three wheeled bicycle and was
custume built for my purpose. The bicycle has strenghtened my legs so much that I
am able to walk much better. In fact my general health is much better than it has
been in many years, so Of course I lay most of it to my bicycle. There is a new
shopping center down at 104th & College Ave(in Homed Place) which includes a large
supermarket known as Joe O'Maley's. This market has the most up-to-date furnishings
incuding carpet over the entire store. Of course I can ride down there and get most
of our grocerirs since most of their prices compares to any A & P. Kroger or Standard.
There is also a modern pharmacy in the center known as Hays plus several doctors &
dentists offices, so it seems to me that Home Place is really growing.

I still go to the Cerebral Palsy Clinic on Mondays, and sometimes on Wednesdays this
summer, and of course I always go swimming over in the big pool at the Union Building
at 5 o-clock on Monday afternoon. A bunch of girls selected from varioys high schools
of Marion and surrounding counties and known at "Teen Tonics" come in and volenteer
their service as assistents to the staff for the C.P. patients at the clinic, and
each one has a Teen Tonic with him in the pool plus several life guards and other
members of the staff. After our swimming we have dinner back at the Rotary Building
then about 8 o-clock the drivers of The Red Cross comes after us and takes us home.
A busy but very enjoyable Monday. Oh-yes I still write the Home Place News items
for the Noblesville Daily Ledger. When I come home on Monday I usualy do a lot of
my typing on the news. One reason is because the swimming has a general effect on
my co-orination, and I seem to be able to do better work

I guess you knew mother went to ExPo 67 the middle of June. She went on a six day
conducted Greyhound Bus Tour and sure had a wonderful trip. Of course she would
have wished for your mother to go with her, but the eye surgery sort of changed their
plans.

Well I had better close and get this in the mail box. I think I'll take it down to
the shopping center and mail, so so-long for this time

                                   Your Cousin

                                   Don Howard

Letter from Cousin Donald Howard,
who had cerebral palsy and was born May 18, 1921

SECOND HONEYMOON

October 1, (my uncelebrated birthday), my plans were established for Japan. I would be physician-in-charge of a medical flight from Tan Son Nhut AF Base to Tokyo.

October 2, I met Arlene in Tokyo at the Sanyo Hotel. At the Tokyo airport, Arlene saw that some soldiers were going to the Sanyo Hotel, and she rode with them to the hotel where we met.

October 3, we took the train to Kyoto and visited the Kiyomigue shrine, the Ryōzen Kannon Temple, and the Heian Shrine. We stayed at The Court of Three Sisters. The first night I took a Japanese bath without Arlene because she was still on Indiana time. We bought some toys for Phillip.

The Ryōzen Kannon was a war memorial commemorating the dead of the Pacific War in Eastern Kyoto. The concrete and steel statue of the Statue of the Bodhisattva Avalokiteśvara was unveiled June 8, 1955. The statue was 80 ft. high and weighed approximately 500 tons.

From the Three Sister we took a train to a boat to Mikimoto Island and watched pearl divers. We bought some pearl jewelry to take to the states. When we got back in Tokyo, I had some delicious raw oysters at a local restaurant that was recommended to us. We visited the Imperial Palace and the Imperial Hotel. When the building had burnt, American Architect Frank Lloyd Wright designed the replaced main building.

October 13, I got the last seat on the 10:30 PM flight from Tokyo and got in Saigon at 4:00 AM. There were six GIs ahead of me for my flight, and with luck, they didn't show up. By the time I got to my BOQ, it was 5:00 AM, so I didn't get much sleep before I went to the lab.

October 15, the rain wouldn't stop. We had three feet of water around the lab. I got cheese from Sister Louise and husband, Bob Walker, and some delicious corn crackers from Brother Bill. I got food snacks from the states every week or two.

October 23, I took a shower in a trickle of water. Winter was in the air. Our meeting in Japan cost around $2,000. I got a letter from Arlene that the pearls we bought in Japan arrived.

October 27, I got a package of raisins, nuts, etc. from Aunt Amelia. Brother Bill sent a 3 lb. package of nuts, and it arrived after three weeks.

Kiyomigue Shrine and Statue of the Bodhisattva Avalokiteśvara

Mikimoto Pearl Divers

Imperial Hotel building, designed by F.L. Wright

Arlene, Ginza District, Tokyo

Arlene at Heinan Shrine

Japanese train station

Court of Three Sisters

RETURN TO ACTION VIETNAM

October 29, I was called into the colonel's office, who was in-charge of the lab and was suspended <u>as chief of pathology</u>. The lab's first sergeant complained that I was three days late (AWOL) on returning from Japan. The colonel said he wasn't going to fine me but was going to remove me as chief of pathology for an indefinite period. My roommate, Bill Illig, took my place.

October 30, I wrote a letter to Dr. V.A. Salvadorini, a Reno pathologist, asking about positions in Reno.

November 3, I got a package from my Aunt Amelia with dried fruit, nuts, etc. I got a book from Bill Sohn. I was watching a lot of lousy movies.

November 5, I put two cans of beer in the refrigerator and within two hours they were gone. <u>I didn't know who had sticky fingers, GIs, Koreans, or both.</u>

November 8, Dr. Charles Larson (my mentor at Tacoma General Hospital) told me about an autopsy he did in Germany during WWII where a GI was shot directly through the anus. I had the exact same situation in Vietnam. A lieutenant was crawling through elephant (tall) grass with his unit. He was found dead and unit's doctor, Captain Jim Fulpert, who just happened to be a classmate at IUSOM, couldn't find a cause of death and sent the body to us for an autopsy. Apparently, they didn't examine the seat of the lieutenant's pants.

November 8 continued, the lieutenant was shot directly through the anus, there were no other wounds.

I sent photos to Dr. Charles Larson, who described a similar event in WWII. Since he was shot from behind, it most likely was by one of our soldiers, or was it by the enemy? I never heard back if it was a homicide, an accident, or KIA. Years later Jim Fulpert practiced in Carson City.

At a party our Reno lab held for general practitioners, he asked me if I remembered the case. I didn't think to ask him if the shooter was identified.

November 11, I did an autopsy on a special forces soldier who was in his quarters when another soldier was coming in from a search and destroy mission in the jungle. The soldier in his quarters said, "I bet you can't shoot me". He was wrong, He was killed on a "Dare".

November 15, I put a lock on my office door as things were being stolen in the lab.

November 21, I did an autopsy on a CIA pilot from Holland, who crashed on takeoff. They were paid around $50,000 per year and could bring their families with them.

November 28, I got a hush-hush murder. A Cambodian working for the CIA was shot in the back of the head. All identification was removed from the body. The CIA didn't want anybody to know he was dead. He apparently was killed by one of our men.

December 9, not much had been going on for the past week. My roommate, Bill Illig, was in bed sick. Al Rieser got into an argument with Ed Katibah, who went into Rieser's lab and ordered Rieser's GIs around. Al also got shot at when he was in a helicopter, so he no longer flew.

December 10, I went into the shop in Cholon where I bought a vase for Arlene, and the clerk asked me if I would buy some Dial soap for her at the PX. I got a letter from Fred Laubscher who opted to enlist for three years and go to Europe. He was not having a great time.

December 14, the 9th Med Lab's CO decided I had been punished enough and reinstated me as chief of pathology.

December 16, everyone in the lab was coming down with Upper Respiratory Infections (URIs). So far, I had been spared. I got a letter from unhappy Tacoma friend, Dave Lucas, who avoided the military and joined the U.S. Public Health for three years.

December 17, I finally got the URI, but it was mild. I saw a suspense movie. At the climax the movie film sizzled and burnt. I will never know how it ended. Christmas was just going to be another day, although a lab party was planned.

December 26, one of the GIs in the lab got caught smoking pot. He faked TB by planting TB organisms in his sputum and he also lied about having a bleeding ulcer. It looks like he will do anything to get out of here. We were getting a fourth pathologist. Since we were only authorized for three pathologists, he would be sent to an outlying facility.

I had done 111 autopsies in 250 days—since I had been here. This did not include autopsies done by my two partners, which were equal to mine. This is approximately 300 autopsies in 250 days.

December 29, GI murdered a VN girl in Vung Tau. I had one of the other pathologists do the autopsy. I could have gone to Cam Rahn Bay to pick up some camera equipment for the lab, but I had one of my pathologists pick it up. The 9th Med Lab's photo department was under pathology.

December 31, I got a raise from $611 base pay to $645. I am going to be rich when I leave the army.

January 1, 1968, I always thought that Sohns were German. Well, let me correct you. My next-door BOQ neighbor was Korean, and he called me, "brother". Sohn is also a Korean clan, and they pronounce it like we do. The Germans pronounce it "Zone". Sohn is also a common Jewish name in New York City. So, what am I?

January 2, we had Niagara Falls outside our window, The water reservoir was running over, and no one was taking care of it.

January 8, I had eight GIs in pathology helping with autopsies etc., when we only needed four. Pathologist Al Garib worked in lab under me for a couple of months. He was as crazy and uncontrollable; he rode a motorcycle with a pistol around town hoping to encounter a VC. We got letters from his creditors in Monterey. One could tell where he had been by looking at the names of owners of books in his possession due to his sticky fingers. One of my books would probably find its way into his fingers.

January 11, I went to Da Nang to testify on an autopsy in a murder case where two

merchant marines killed a VN bar girl on the beach. The trial was postponed so I would have to go back. On the way up we stopped at Pleiku and got down in a ditch by the runway to avoid a plane that was crash-landing because it couldn't lower its wheels. In Da Nang I stayed at Red Beach, a marine base that was the jumping-off point to fight in the DMZ.

The most emotional part of the trip was seeing the mountain range where my roommate at SFGH, Bruce Farrell, was killed. As a navy flight surgeon, he went out on rescue missions. He was killed when a second helicopter came in on top of his and killed all aboard. After that mission the admiral issued an order that no doctors were to go on any future rescue missions. Years later, in 1992 when I was at Johns Hopkins SOM, I visited the VN wall in Washington D.C. where the names of those killed in VN are listed. Bruce's name was at the foot of the wall where those first killed in VN were listed. It was very emotional for me to see his name on the D.C. wall.

On the flight back to Saigon, I was doctor-in-charge of a GI, who accidentally set off a phosphorous grenade and received third degree burns over 65% of his body.

I did an autopsy on a GI who was standing guard in a watch tower when he was struck by lightning. The only visible injury was a torn boot from the lightning blast.

Michael Medawar Jr., who graduated from Louisiana State University SOM in 1961, was stationed with us at the 9th Medical Lab for a short time. After the military, he practiced in Tulsa, Oklahoma with Bill Illig.

January 15, 1968, I reached the $10,000 savings limit allowed for Vietnam. I was having trouble with Al Garib. He couldn't finish his cases due to lack of training. He was having trouble diagnosing slides. The number of GIs in Saigon was down, and the bars were complaining because sales were down.

January 21, we had a little fire at the lab. One of the flares they throw out of planes to light the perimeter at Tan Son Nhut AFB fell into our parking lot, and its parachute caught fire.

January 22, I received a letter from <u>Dr. Owen Bolstad that his group had an opening for a pathologist in Reno.</u> My IU classmate, Dr. Ron Cudek, said <u>Salvadorini's group had an opening.</u>

January 25, a friend who just got back from Hong Kong said a room at the Hilton cost $10 a day. I hadn't done an autopsy since Christmas. We had four pathologists and two only did autopsies. One didn't want to do surgicals because he didn't feel capable; I agreed.

January 28, the sound of firecrackers was constant. I guess this was in preparation for Tet.

January 29, I got my orders to return to Oakland, California, no later than April 13.

January 31, there were rumors of VC activity. I wouldn't go to Hong Kong the next day as planned because TSN AFB was closed, and we were locked in the BOQ. I took photos of the Tet air strikes from my window.

I got a call from our CO that one of the lab's GIs got shot by a VC while in a jeep. I examined him and there were typical burns from the muzzle of a rifle. It was obvious that he held the muzzle of the gun near his arm, pulled the trigger and got the burn.

I did 111 autopsies. Unfortunately, I did not record the exact period when these autopsies were done, but they were done by early January 1968. Ninety (81%) were not directly related to combat. A frequent cause of death was due to complications from battle wounds (21 of the 111).

Of the remaining 90, forty-nine (54.4%) were the result of aircraft accidents and most of these were helicopter crashes with resulting intense fire. This is not surprising, pilots flew fast, low to avoid ground fire, in bad weather, and sometimes without maintenance.

VC was able to sneak approximately 1,000 fighters into Saigon. I watched the war while sipping scotch in my air-conditioned room. Even though we were locked in, Korean soldiers next door climbed over the barricades around the BOQ to join the battle.

Captain A.P. Sohn's 111 Consecutive Autopsies (Typical Period)
(U.S. Military deaths, not killed in action)

49 (44%) Helicopter accidents

21 (19%) Complications from battle wounds

10 (9%) Heart disease

7 (6%) Accidental drowning in rice paddies

6 (5%) Vehicular accidents

3 (3%) Suicides

3 (3%) Homicides

3 (3%) Gunshot wounds, possible accidents

2 (2%) Alcohol intoxication

2 (2%) Parachute accidents

1 (1%) Burn

1 (1%) Malaria

1 (1%) Alleged fall, probably homicide (See page 17)

1 (1%) Lightning strike (See pages 28, 31 & 35)

Plane crash landing at Pleiku

APS "Battle-Ready"

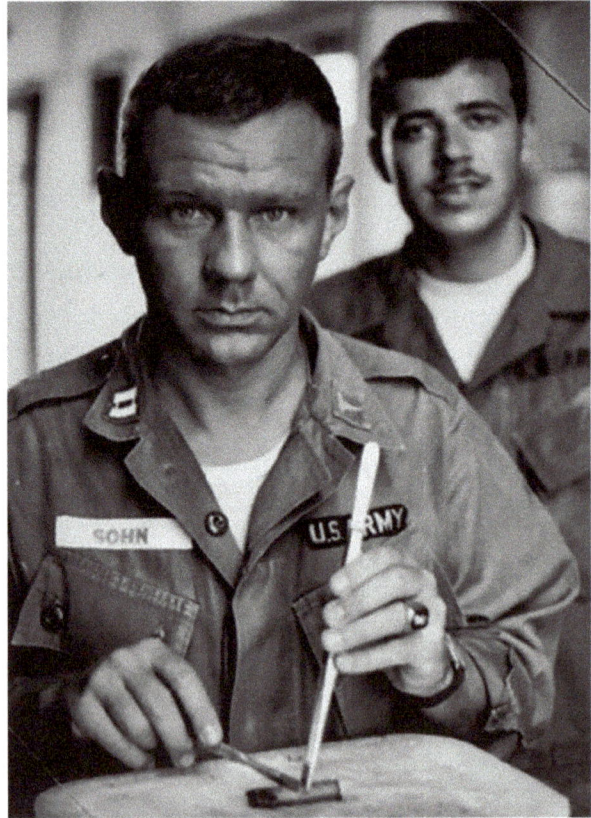

APS dissecting "fake" specimen (cigar)

Mountain Range where Dr. Bruce Farrell was killed (taken from Marine Red Beach)

Path. Asst. Harlan Abbott at 9th Med Lab, 1967

APS at Da Nang's Marine Red Beach

APS diagnosing a microscopic slide

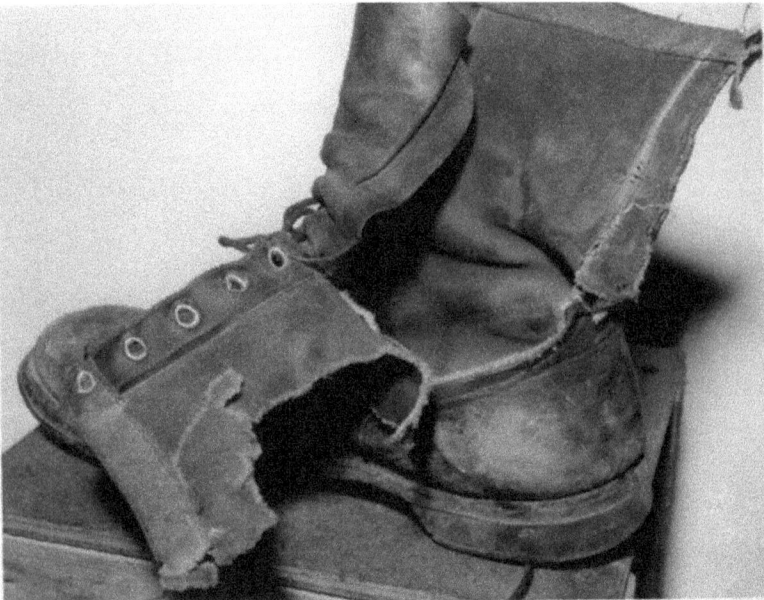

Boot of GI struck by lightning

SAIGON ON FIRE

February 1, the VC made a few technical errors when they started the Tet offensive. They didn't hit the power plant that supplies Saigon and they holed up villages thinking we wouldn't hit civilian areas. We bombed the "hell out" of the villages where they thought they were secure. <u>Parts of Saigon were on fire.</u>

February 2, we heard the lab was secure and hadn't been hit.

Saigon "On Fire" (Photos from my Lucky BOQ window)

Saigon "On Fire" (Photos from my Lucky BOQ window)

Saigon "On Fire" & Flares being dropped (Photos from my Lucky BOQ window)

RELAXING HONG KONG

February 4, I left at 3:30 PM to Tan Son Nhut AFB with an armed guard to fly to Hong Kong for R & R. We passed many burnt houses and shops. The VC had been quietly infiltrating the city for months. We had one GI at the 9th Med Lab killed by VC. He was living with a VN girl and didn't get the word of the invasion. I heard that four GIs who lived in our BOQ were killed.

February 6, I was safely in the Hong Kong Hilton. I dreaded going back to Saigon. I stayed in Hong Kong for 5 days and spent a lot of $ on gifts for family. I also bought a tiger-skin rug. I took a boat out to the Tai Pak restaurant and had a fantastic dinner.

My dinner menu

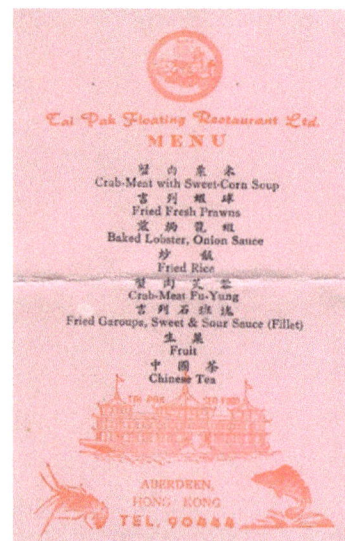

Tai Pak Restaurant

APS, top of Hong Kong Mountain by train

Hong Kong harbor from mountain top

8 ft. 6 in. tiger skin rug

7 ft. x 3 ft. Japanese panel painting

In Hong Kong I bought a tiger skin rug. I also bought jewelry, cameras, and electronic equipment for friends. I bought the Japanese panel painting at the Saigon PX.

FINAL STOP SAIGON

February 9, when I got back to TSN AFB, I got a ride from military police to the morgue. From there I called the lab, and they sent a jeep. <u>Because life in Saigon was precarious, we were sleeping in the lab.</u>

February 11, fighting was going on around Saigon, and we stayed in the BOQ for three days. **Our surgical load was down to six a day and we usually had 20-30.**

February 21, Action around Saigon had been sporadic for the past 10 days.

Colonel J. Hinton Baker awarding the Bronze Star to APS

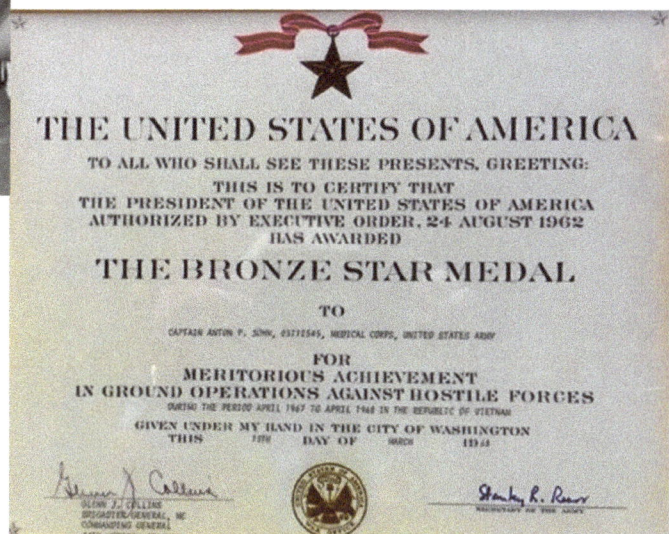

THE UNITED STATES OF AMERICA

TO ALL WHO SHALL SEE THESE PRESENTS, GREETING:
THIS IS TO CERTIFY THAT
THE PRESIDENT OF THE UNITED STATES OF AMERICA
AUTHORIZED BY EXECUTIVE ORDER, 24 AUGUST 1962
HAS AWARDED

THE BRONZE STAR MEDAL

TO

CAPTAIN ANTON P. SOHN, 05313545, MEDICAL CORPS, UNITED STATES ARMY

FOR

MERITORIOUS ACHIEVEMENT
IN GROUND OPERATIONS AGAINST HOSTILE FORCES

DURING THE PERIOD APRIL 1967 TO APRIL 1968 IN THE REPUBLIC OF VIETNAM

GIVEN UNDER MY HAND IN THE CITY OF WASHINGTON
THIS   DAY OF   MARCH   1968

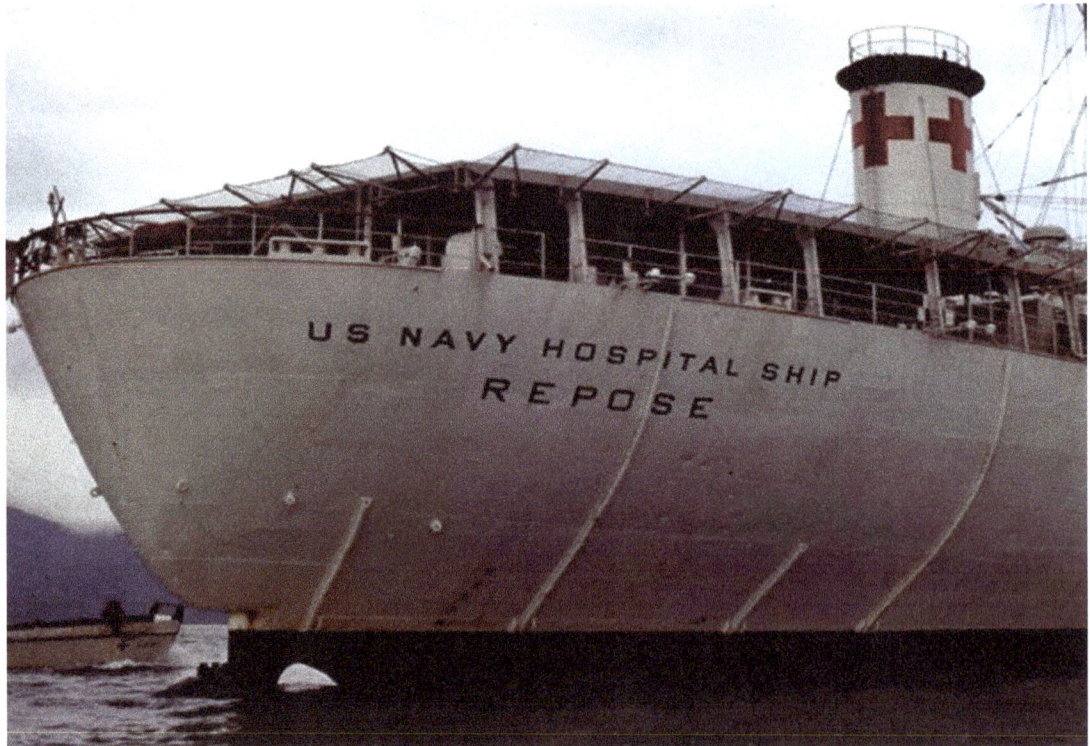

APS on U.S. Navy Hospital Ship Repose at Da Nang

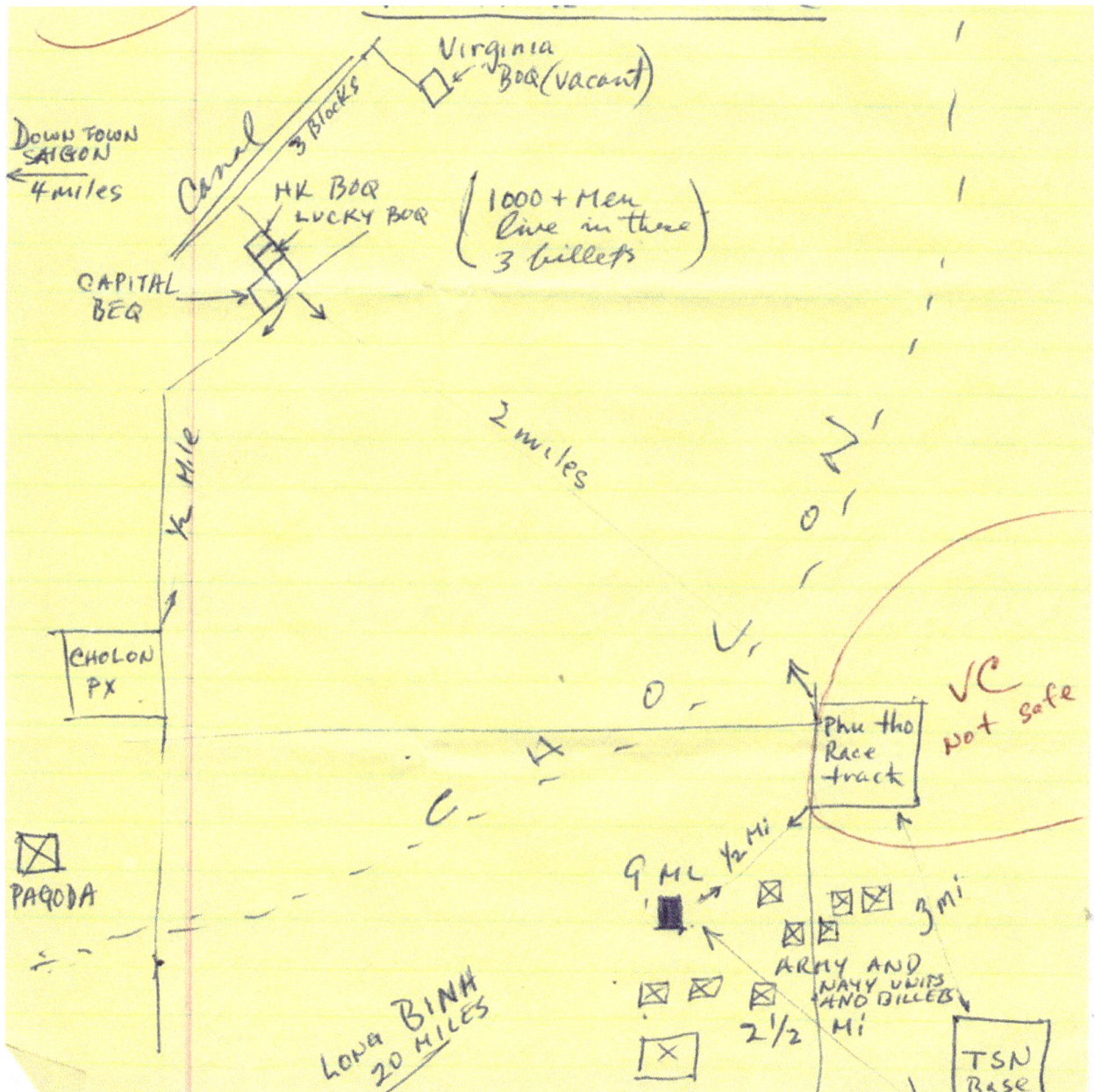

My "Little World" in Saigon

Phu Tho Racetrack had a grandstand where the VC set up headquarters for the Tet offensive, which lasted from January to February. Tet is the VN New Year. To get to the 9th Med Lab, we drove in front of the Phu Tho Racetrack with our heads down.

February 22, I was in Da Nang and the place was safer than Saigon even though it was near the border with North VN. I went to the *U.S. Navy Hospital Ship Repose* for dinner at the invitation of the captain of the ship. I sipped Cherry Herring after dinner. The meals were better than in Saigon. I was staying at Red Beach Marine Base to testify on a murder case.

February 24, I went on the stand this morning in Da Nang, and the defense didn't cross examine me as the case was pretty cut and dry. Two merchant marines killed a VN bar girl. It was the first-time civilians have been tried in a military court in VN. The trip gave me insight as to how marines fight. It was entirely different than you or I think. They want to get hit, so they can fight. <u>I was asked by a marine if I wanted to go on a search and destroy mission.</u> He said he would put me next to the machine gunner where I would be safe. <u>Don't spend too much time figuring out what my reply was.</u>

March 4, I haven't been out of the BOQ for four days—watching movies every night and sunbathing during the day while listening to music. The next night I would spend at the lab as the officer-of-the-day.

March 8, I ran into Dr. Phil Weinstein, an IUSOM classmate, at the 3rd Field Hospital. He invited me to his quarters for cocktails. I was unable to find time to meet him.

March 10, we got another pathologist at the 9th Med Lab.

March 30, I received the Bronze Star, National Service Defense Medal, Vietnam Campaign Medal W/Device, and Vietnam Service Medal from Colonel Hinton J. Baker, CO, 9th Med Lab.

HELLO CIVILIAN LIFE

April 11, I flew from Tan Son Nhut AFB to Oakland, California and was honorably discharged. The colonel in-charge told me that if I joined the reserves, they would pay my way to Indianapolis. <u>I politely declined and told him I would pay my own way</u>. From Indianapolis, Arlene and I flew to Reno, where I accepted a position with Dr. Salvadorini's group, Physicians Consulting Laboratories and resumed a civilian life.

I declined an invitati0n to join Dr. Bolstad's group because it involved flying to outlying labs, and I wanted to be based in a hospital laboratory.

I returned to civilian life in the 1968, and we moved to Reno to join Physicians Consulting labs (PCL), which consisted of five pathologists. A second group, Western Pathologists Associates (WPL), which included Drs. Owen Bolstad, Don Schieve, and three pathologists based in California was also based in Reno. In 1971 PCL approached WPL to jointly purchase a $30,000 twelve-test chemistry analyzer. As a result, the two groups merged and formed a clinical laboratory at 888 Willow Street, a two-story, 16,000-square-foot building.

The merged group had 140 employees and twelve pathologists who served twenty hospitals. In 1993 we sold the lab to Allied Clinical Laboratories which joined LabCorp.

In 1977 Dr. Salvadorini retired as director of Washoe Medical Center's (WMC-now Renown Regional Medical Center) laboratory, and on September 1, 1977, the hospital's board of directors appointed me laboratory director. I had the good fortune to be involved with a group of physicians who were leaders in local and state politics. Both of my partners, Dr. V.A. Salvadorini and Dr. Jack Callister, were past presidents of the Washoe County Medical Society and the Nevada State Medical Association (NSMA). However, becoming president of Reno Surgical Society was my first step in medical politics.

The society's membership required each member to give a talk and pay for dinner on a rotating basis. We also had invited speakers. Dr. Salvadorini was acquainted with Dr. Charles Larson and hosted him as a speaker. When it became my time to give a talk, I decided to discuss blood alcohol levels.

At a previous meeting I asked ten volunteers to have a blood alcohol (BA) drawn and keep track of how many drinks they had. I asked another group of ten to have a blood alcohol drawn, but they were not told beforehand to keep a count of their drinks. I brought two lab technicians to the meeting to draw blood alcohols.

The individuals who were told to keep track of the number of drinks had BAs that correlated with the number of drinks they consumed. The individuals who were not told had BAs showing they underestimated their number of drinks by one half. <u>Conclusion: after two or more drinks most alcohol drinkers don't remember how many drinks they consume.</u>

In 1977 I was elected President of Washoe County Medical Society and in 1984 I was elected president of the Nevada State Medical Association (NSMA).

In 1984 Dean Bob Daugherty of the University of Nevada School of Medicine (UNSOM), now University of Nevada Reno School of Medicine (UNRSOM) appointed me chairman of pathology. Dr. Ritzlin, Dr. Parks, and Course Coordinator Ken Maehara were the backbone of the department. Later, Dean Tom Schwenk named the history of medicine museum, "Anton and Arlene Great Basin History of Medicine Museum".

One of my first actions was to create a history program in the department. At the Indiana University School of Medicine, I was required to write a history of medicine research paper for pathology. I brought this tradition to the Nevada's School of Medicine and required students in pathology to write a 1,500-word literature research paper on a history of medicine subject.

Dr. Owen Bolstad and I also founded a quarterly history of medicine bulletin. I named it *Greasewood*, after a desert plant that Native American Piute and Shoshone had used for thousands of years to treat aliments. Owen added *Tablettes*, the French word for tablet, to give the bulletin's name sophistication. In 2022, *Greasewood Tablettes* is in its 32nd year of publication.

The pathology department's history of medicine program also includes Greasewood Press, which has published sixteen books, an oral history program with over 120 histories, the Great Basin History of Medicine Museum, and the Doctors Hood Library. The museum and library are located at the north end of the school's Savitt Library on the School of Medicine's Reno campus.

To further my knowledge of the history of medicine, in 1991, I took a one-year-sabbatical at Johns Hopkins Institute of the History of Medicine in Baltimore to advance my knowledge and do research at the Library of Congress.

In 2009, I retired from practice and the University of Nevada, Reno School of Medicine, but I maintained my medical license and continued to do forensic consultations.

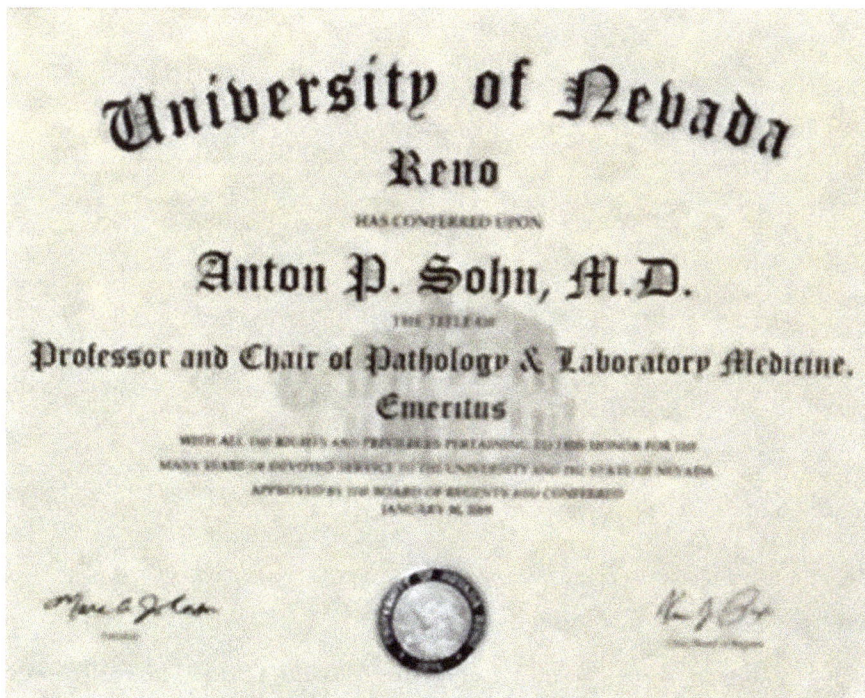

Emeritus certificate, 2009

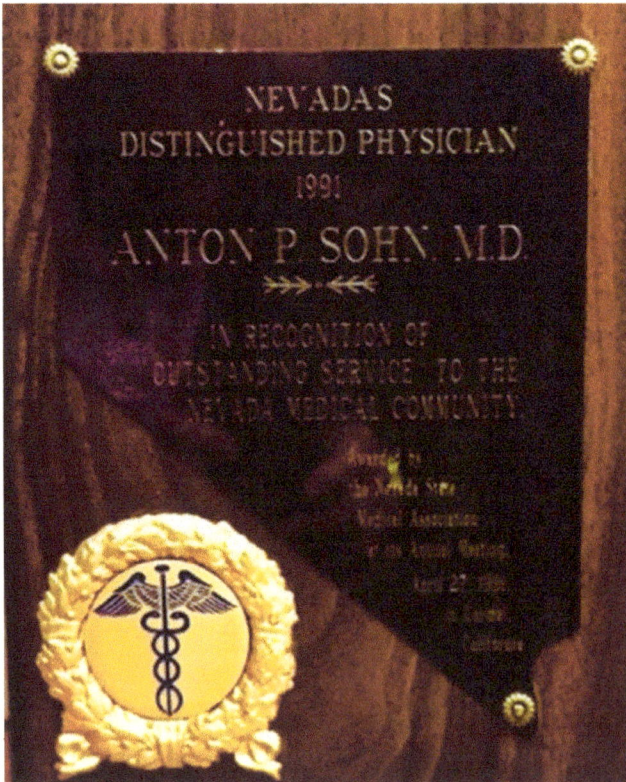

Nevada's Distinguished Physician and President's Award for Service

Kristin with Grandma Helen Hedegard, Oct. 1, 1997

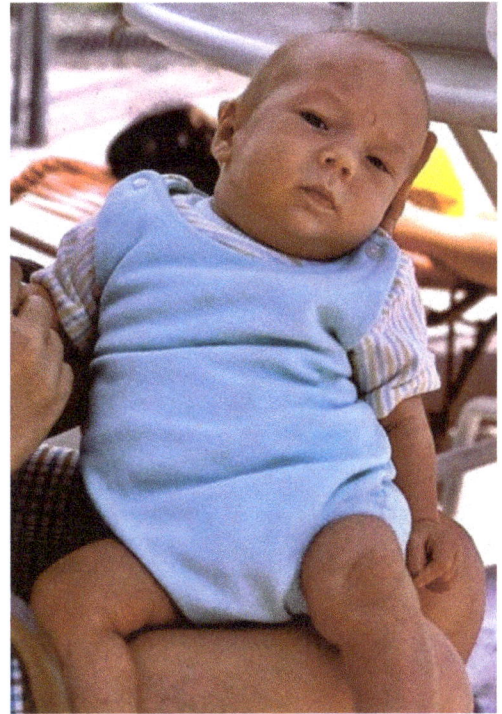

Eric, April 14, 1969

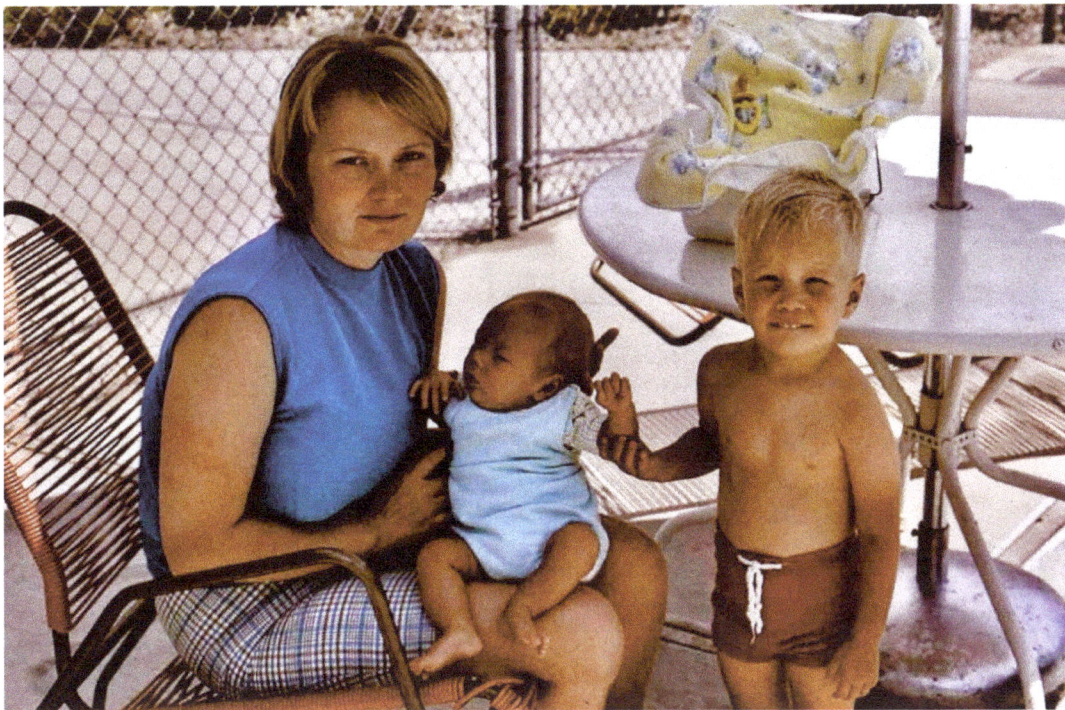

Arlene, Eric, and Phil, April 4, 1969

APS, NSMA Presidency, 1984

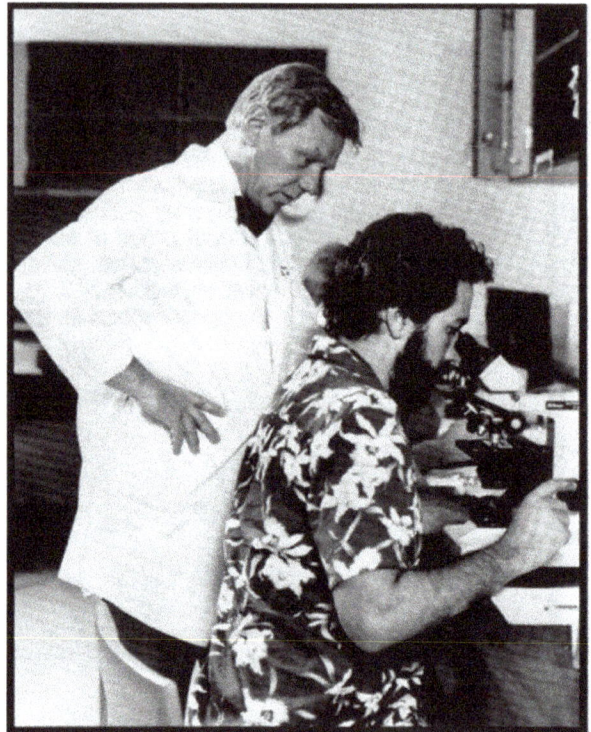

APS teaching a student, 1986

Drs. APS and Jack Talsma, 1976

SOCIETY OFFICERS -Dr. Anton P. Sohn, left, and Dr. Jack E. Talsma, has cheerful looks following the annual membership meeting of the Washoe County Medical Society. Dr. Talsma was installed as the president and Dr. Sohn, a Washoe Medical center pathologist, was named present-elect of the society.

APS, WMC lab director, 1977

APS, Great Basin History of Medicine Museum at UNRSOM, 2002

Phil wearing hat I bought in Vietnam for him, 1969

II: Veterinary Medicine 1967-8, Captain Warren D. Myers

Warren D. Myers graduated from Penn State University in 1961 with a BS. In 1965 he graduated from the University of Pennsylvania with a VMD. He was drafted into the army in 1966 and spent one year at 6th Army Medical Laboratory in San Francisco. In 1967 he was transferred to the 9th Medical Laboratory in Saigon where he served under Major David Huxsoll. After honorable discharge, Warren moved to Vacaville and founded the Vaca Valley Veterinary Hospital.

Warren D. Myers: "The Veterinary Division of the 9th Med Lab provided laboratory and diagnostic support for all veterinary units in Vietnam. This included laboratory training and backup for veterinary personnel in field units that supply guard dogs, tunnel K-9, and sentry guard dogs for the U.S. Army and Air Force.

"Additional support included diagnosis of rabies etc. in suspects using three diagnostic methods: fluorescent antibody, Negri body inclusion pathology and the inoculation of lab mice with suspect inoculum.

"Since positive rabies results approached 33% in suspected cases throughout Vietnam, this was one of the most important responsibilities of the division. When possible, necropsies were done on all K-9 units to provide information with respect to their serviceability and cause of death.

"In Vietnam I did over 100 necropsies on dogs with hip dysplasia. Prior to VN hip dysplasia in dogs was thought to be a disease that did not progress in severity. As a result, dogs trained in Texas were accepted in VN with minimal dysplasia. The air force tried to find clean (grade 0) dogs but had to settle for grade 1 and finally grade 2 in the later stages of the war.

"At University of Pennsylvania, I worked with Dr. Wayne Riser and developed a grading system of 1 to 5 for hip dysplasia. In VN, I found that dogs progressed from grade 1 to grade 5. The stress factor in VN was part of the cause and progression occurred in as little as one year. Ninety percent of the dogs I necropsied had severe dysplasia in

1½ years. As a result of my findings, hip dysplasia in dogs in now known to be a progressive disease.

"To find dogs progressing to Grade 5, changed the thinking of the veterinary minds on hip dysplasia.

"Rabies is a disease that was seen in Vietnamese civilians and was almost nonexistent in the U.S. Military. I tested over 100 suspected dogs of rabies at the 9th Med Lab with a 33% positive rate. There were thousands of human exposures to positive suspects (most all canine) with almost no infections. It appears that humans are somewhat resistant to rabies. There are at least three reasons; lack of viremia, better wound cleaning, and heredity that prevent infections."

Captain Myers and Major David Huxoll

Captain Myers at 35th Evac. Lab, Vung Tau

Captain Myers treating a sentry dog, Tan Son Nhut Air Force Base

Captain Myers

VN guard at 9th Medical Laboratory

Captain Myers & Navy SEAL at Vung Tau

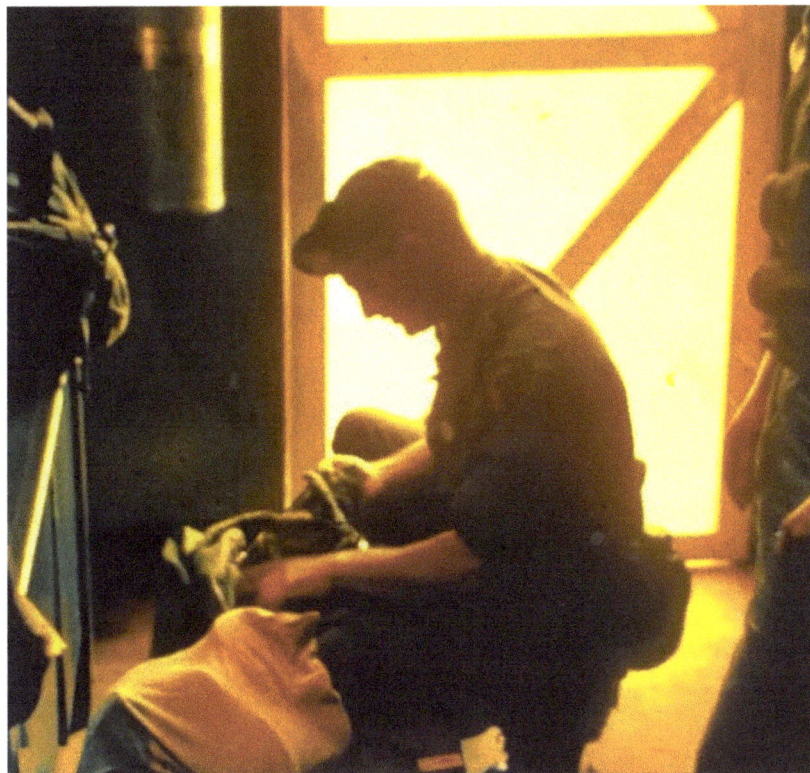

Green Beret on mission from 9th Med Lab

VN cemetery where VC buried ammo for Tet

U.S. Embassy in Saigon

Captain Myers at 35th Evacuation Hospital

III: 7TH SURGICAL HOSPITAL 1967-8, CAPTAIN THOMAS W. BRADY

Thomas W. Brady graduated with an MD in 1963 from the Kansas University School of Medicine (KUSOM). He did a surgical internship at KUSOM and had finished two years of a urology residency when he got drafted in the U.S. Army in 1967. His career in the army started in Fort Jackson, Columbia, South Carolina. In June 1967, he was sent to Vietnam and stationed at the 7th Surgical Mobile Army Hospital (Bien Hoa, Cu Chi, & Xuan Loc) until June 1968. In June 1968, Dr. Brady was sent to Fort Leavenworth to finish his two-year military obligation.

In 1969, he returned to finish his urology residency at KUSOM. In 1970, after visiting a urology group in Ventura, California, he stopped in to visit his Kansas University Phi Delta Theta fraternity brother, Dr. Don Day, in Reno. Dr. Day introduced him to Drs. Carl Sauls and Gordon Nitz. He liked their friendship and practice and joined their Reno urology practice. Dr. Tom Brady practiced 40 years in Reno and died November 17, 2021, at the age of 83.

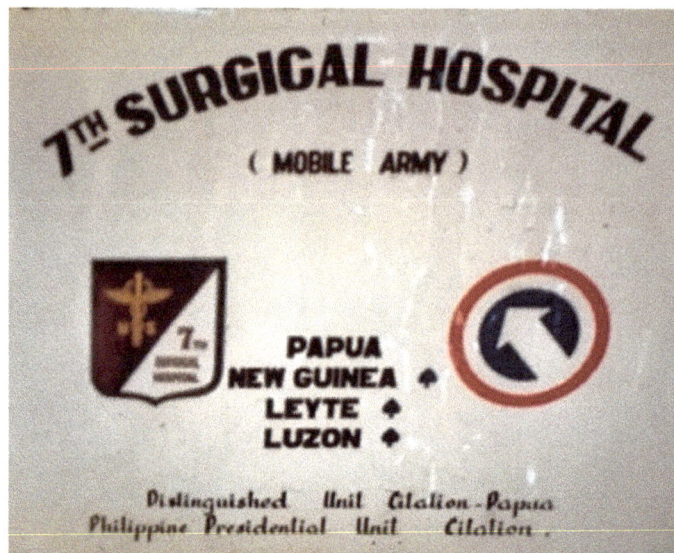

7th Surgical Hospital's campaigns

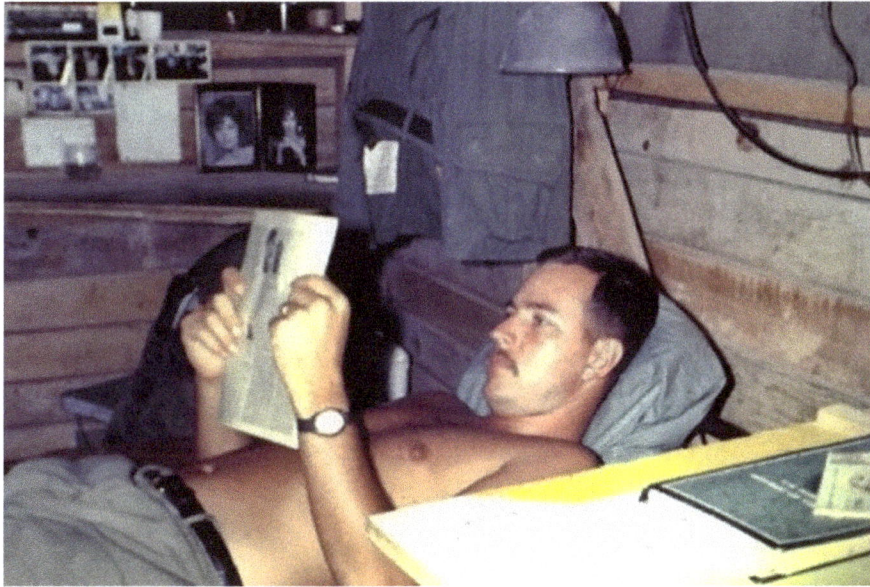

Captain Brady in BOQ

Jeep, wire cutter to prevent crossroad wires

VC prisoner leaving medical clinic

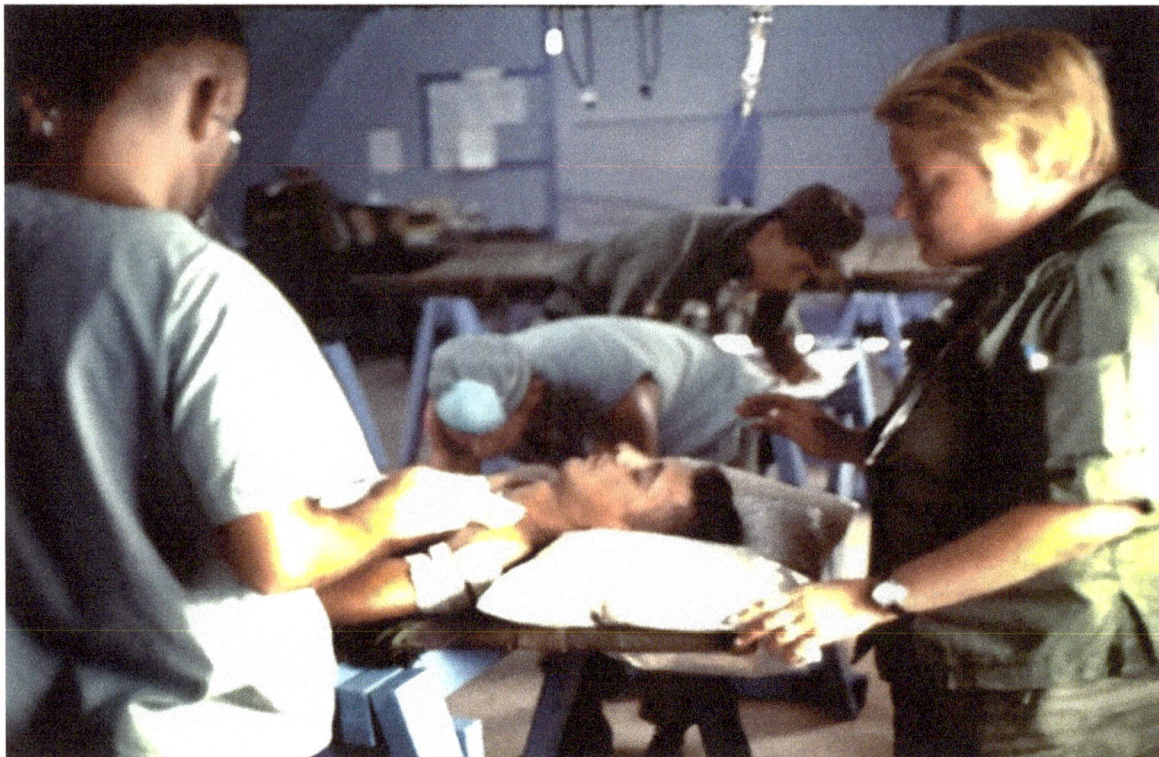

Evaluating patient in pre-op room

Relaxing in the bunker on a sunny afternoon

Captain Brady

Captain Brady on convoy

Captain Brady interacting with Vietnamese children

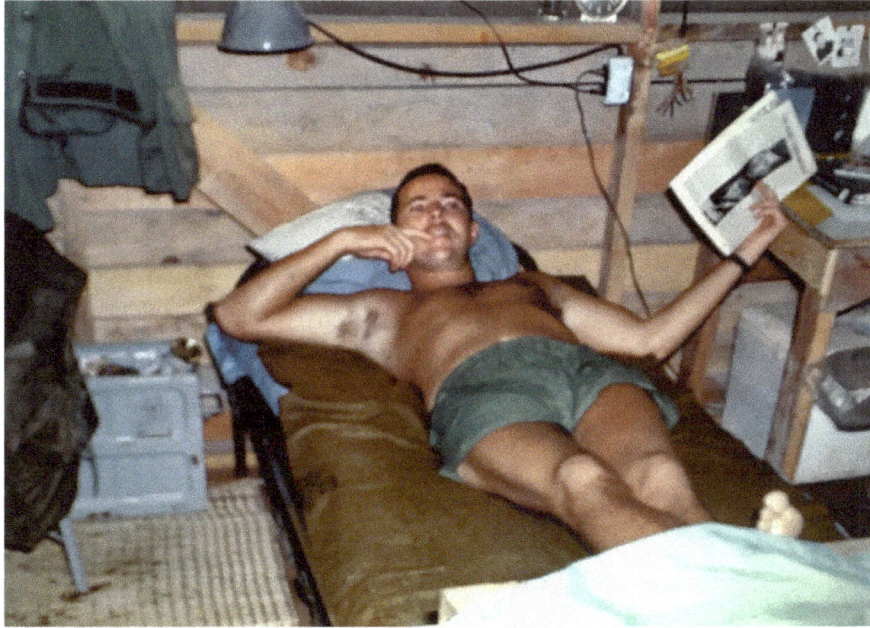

Captain Brady in Cu Chi BOQ

Bob Hope with Miss World entertaining troops at Cu Chi

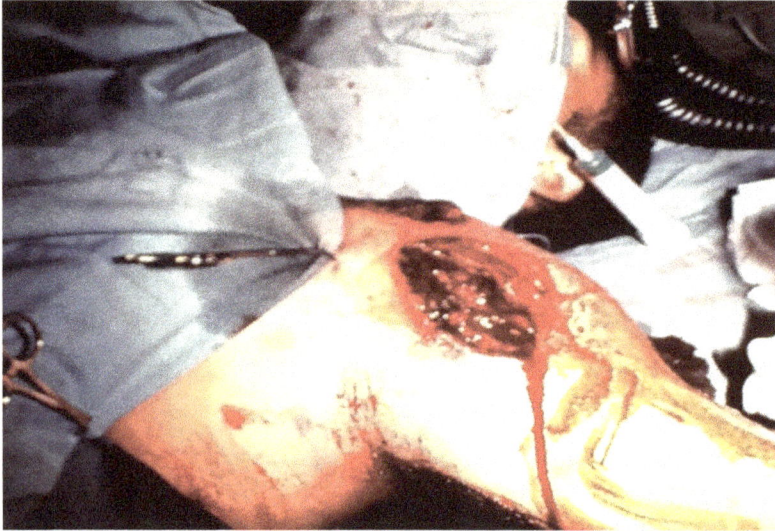

Shoulder wound in OR

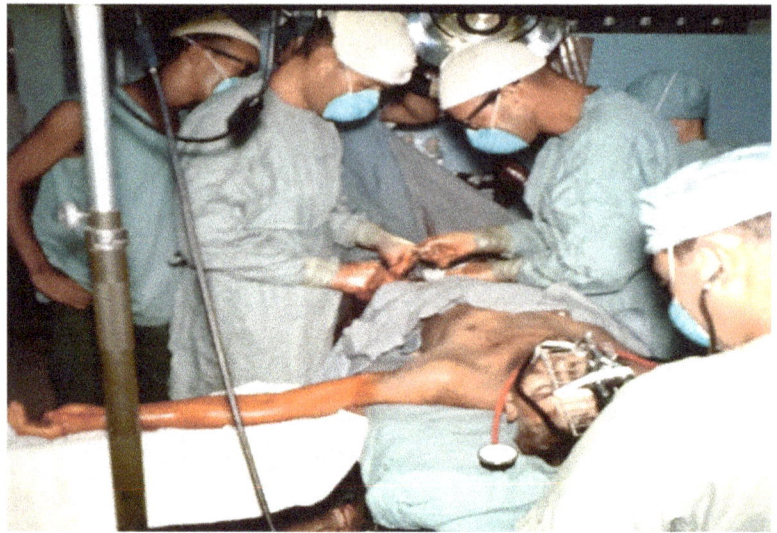

Captain Brady with assistants Scichitand, Hughes, & Wechsler

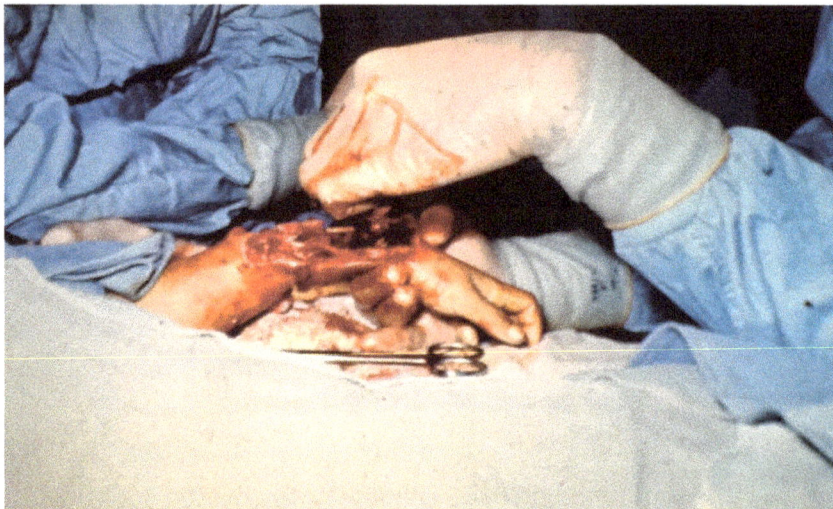

Hand wound surgery in OR

IV: MACV-SOG 1969-70,
NAVY LIEUTENANT RICHARD P. GANCHAN

Richard P. Ganchan: "I graduated from Rice University in 1964 and then went "across the street" to Baylor College of Medicine and graduated with an MD in 1968. 'With manpower needs of the Vietnam war, the Berry Plan gave me the option regarding obligations for military service. I chose to go into service after one year of a Med-Peds internship at the University of Utah. I became a U.S. Navy doctor in July 1969 at the MCRD (Marine Corps Recruiting Depot) in San Diego! The MCRD shared a fence with San Diego airport.

'Talk about a lush assignment! My job was to staff a medical clinic with other docs for marine recruits.' After about eight months, I was informed the navy wanted a volunteer from our group to go to a secretive organization in Vietnam. If no one volunteered, a single doctor would be selected. Well, despite a new wife and a new infant daughter, I volunteered. WHY? Frankly, I was bored with sick-call for 18-year-old guys. I was also curious as to what was happening in Vietnam.

"The press, our government, and protesters resulted in a very chaotic time in our nation. In addition, there was a rumor that the second year of my tour might be on a ship, and I had no desire to be on a ship. 'So, off to Saigon to MACV-SOG (Military Assistance Command Vietnam-Studies and Observation Group). SOG was created to find and monitor NVA (North Vietnamese Army) supply routes in Laos and Cambodia, call in air strikes, and bomb the Hell out of them."

"We had hundreds of SF (Special Forces) guys on TDY (temporary duty) in bases at Ba Me Thout and Kontum in the Central Highlands that were closed to those who had no clearance. Of more interest, these bases also had members of ARVN (Army of the Republic of Vietnam Rangers). The small groups that went on missions included three warrior groups—U.S. Special Forces, ARVN Rangers, and mercenary Montagnards (hill dwelling people of the highlands of Vietnam). At Danang (on the China Sea Coast) we had Navy Seals on Temporary Duty, who had two very fast, heavily armored boats for clandestine etc. missions, of which I was never privy to. However, I was lucky enough to get a ride—55 knots (63 MPH) it was quite a ride!

"We had our own planes (C-130s and C-123's), and five pilots from China Airlines.

"There were PSY-Ops (psychological operations) and other happenings, of which I was never privy to. What then was my job description? Well, it was strictly administrative. I had an office in a five-story air-conditioned office building in Saigon. Under me were an Army Medical Service Lieutenant and a Navy Chief Petty Officer.

"I made frequent trips to the above bases, and I would do inspections of the kitchens. Needless-to-say, Montagnard kitchens never passed inspection. I socialized with the Special Forces and U.S. SEAL medics, who saw many patients with malaria and STDs (Sexually Transmitted Diseases), which they handled quite-well.

"After a 10-hour day in the office, I would drive in my little Datsun sedan in Saigon rush-hour-traffic to Tan Son Nhut AFB, play handball in a very nice handball court (I have a trophy to show for the effort), shower, and go to a BOQ for steak and Schlitz beer. Dr. Treat Cafferata was surgeon at a Saigon military hospital and invited me to dinner one night. He was trying to find out why I was visiting two wounded Montagnards in his hospital. However, I could not tell him the reason.

Meaningful trips during my tour in Vietnam included visits to a Buddhist orphanage and a tour of a leprosy colony manned by Vietnamese nuns. The leprosy colony patients and their families were all Montagnards.

"I visited civilian Dr. Patricia Smith who oversaw an open-air hospital in Kontum for Montagnards. She showed me her hospital with a bottle of Maalox (an antacid to reduce indigestion) in her hand. Among her patients were three infants with tuberculosis. After the two years of military service, I returned to the University of Utah to continue my residency. In 1976, I met Dr. James Atcheson. He was my attending physician for about six weeks when he was a metabolic fellow. He invited me to Reno where I eventually practiced cardiology until my retirement."

Lt. Ganchan's BOQ

Building defense against satchel charges

Lieutenant Ganchan

Lieutenant Ganchan in Saigon and with personal auto

Lt. Ganchan on the beach

Lt. Ganchan at Dak To Long where 361 Americans were killed

Lieutenant Ganchan at an orphanage

Buddhist orphanage

Dak To Long

Leprosy is a contagious disease caused by a bacterium that destroys skin and mucus membranes.

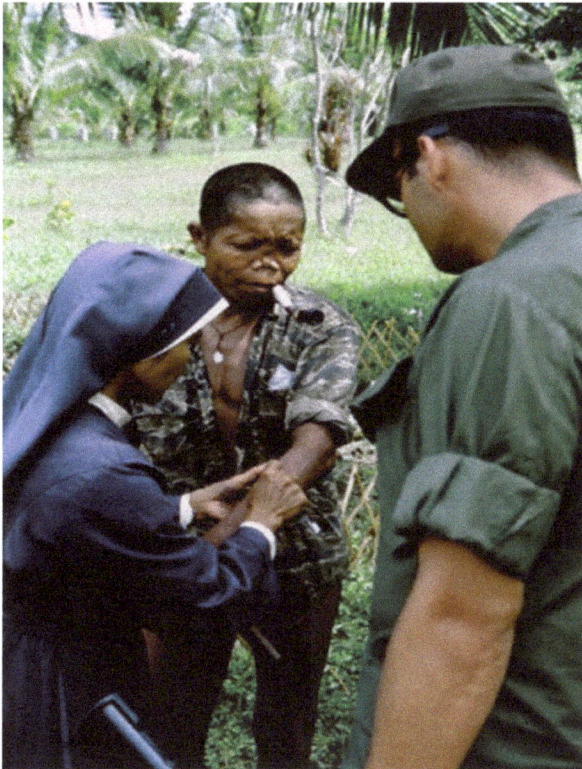

Montagnard with leprosy of the nose

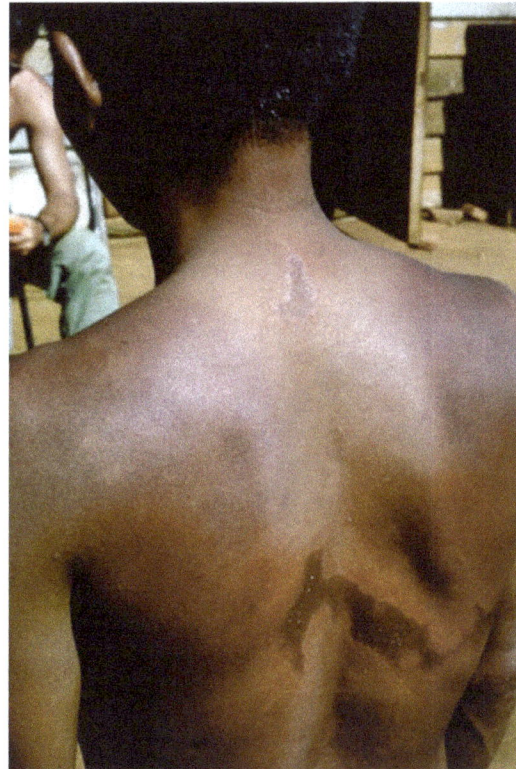

Montagnard with leprosy

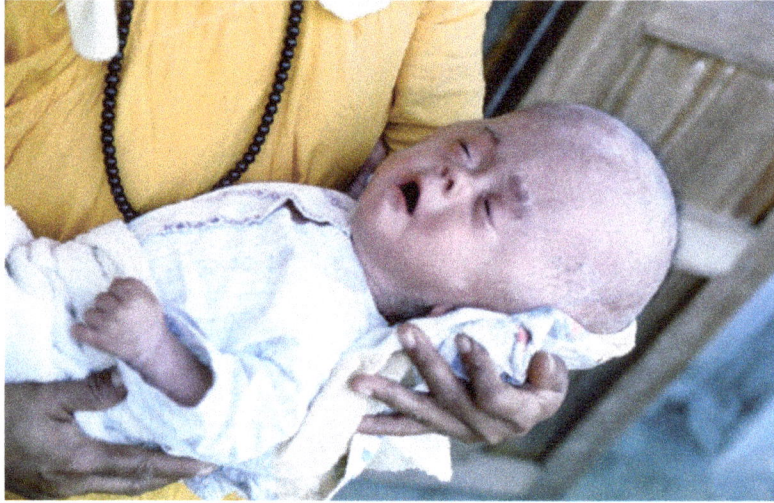

Infant with hydrocephaly

Hydrocephaly is fluid in the head due to a blockage in the brain resulting in head enlargement.

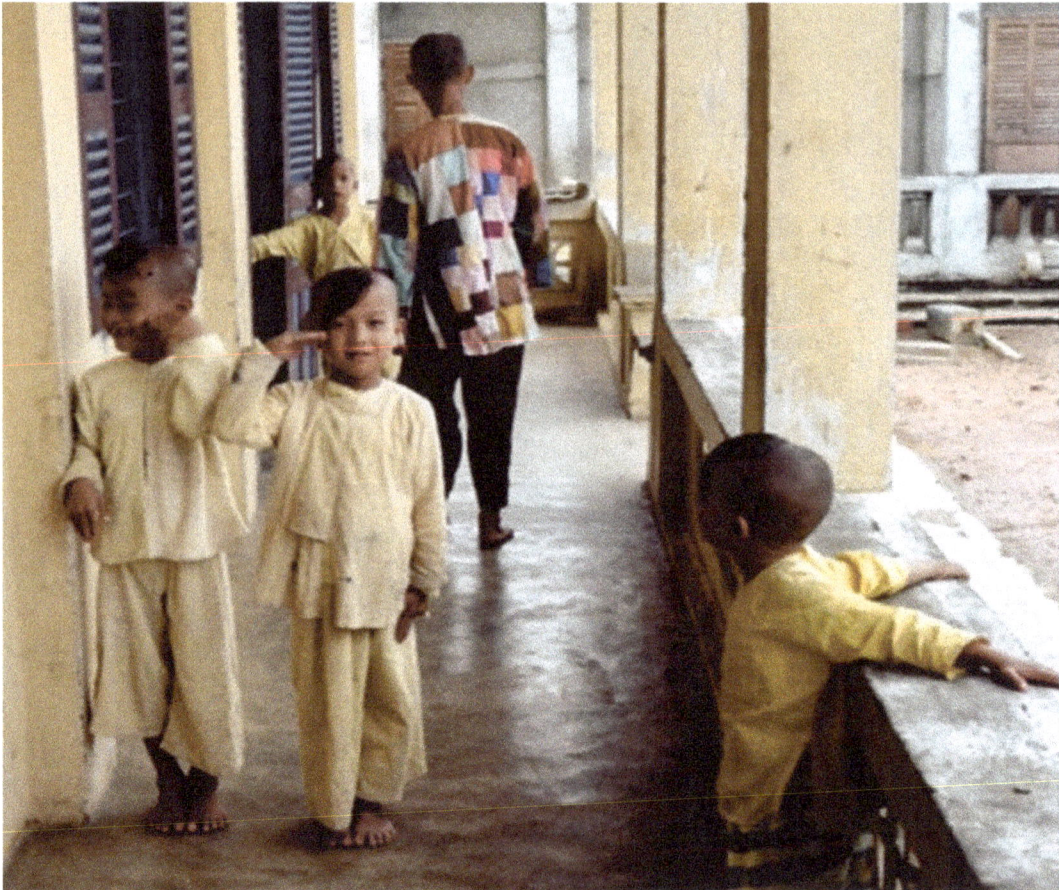

Buddhist orphanage (note military salutes)

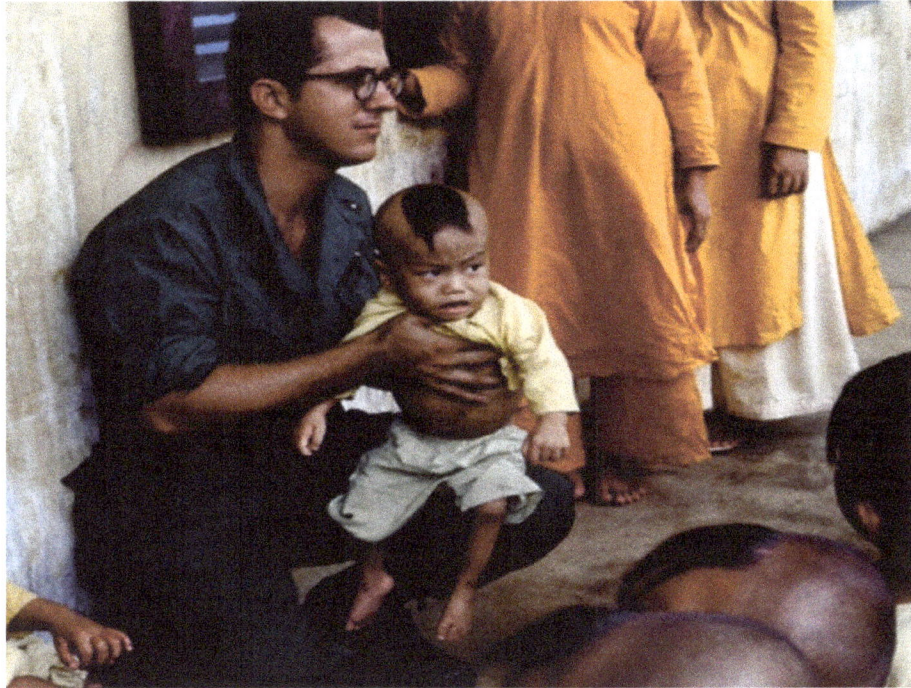

Lt. Ganchan on sick call at the orphanage

"MY 51-WEEK VIETNAM-TOUR-OF-DUTY WAS THE MOST BROADENING YEAR OF MY LIFE. I WILL ALWAYS HAVE THE HIGHEST REGARD FOR OUR NATION'S WARRIORS," DR. RICHARD GANCHAN

POSTSCRIPT:
ARMY 1958-9, 910 MED. CORPSMAN WILLIAM P. SOHN

W.P. 'Bill' Sohn was in the U.S. Army Medical Corps from 1958 to 1959. He joined the army after graduating from Indiana University and did basic training at Fort Leonard Wood, Missouri. He was joined by his friend, Jim Grayson. Bill did medical training at Fort Sam Houston and spent a couple of days at Camp Bullis before reserve training at Fort Benjamin Harrison, Indiana.

CAMP BULLIS

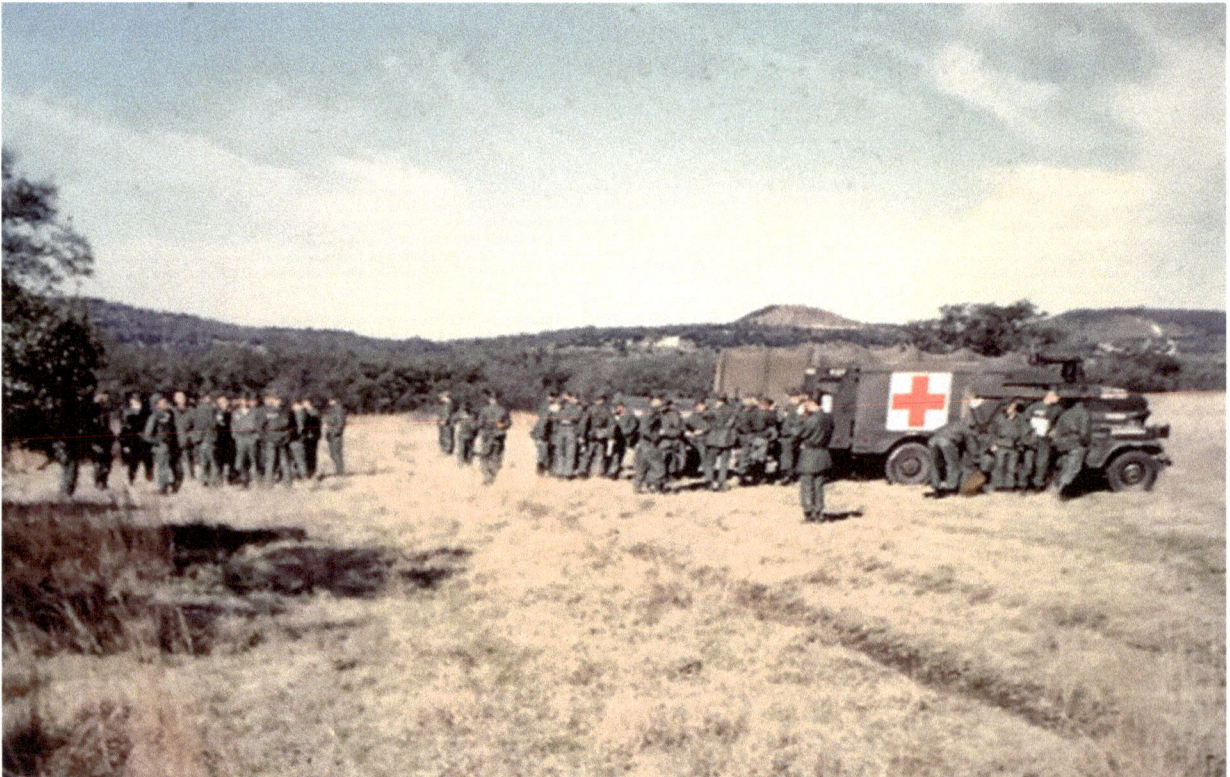

William P. Sohn's medical unit

Jim Grayson and William P. Sohn

Camp Bullis helicopter

NAME INDEX

+_+

A

Abbott, Harlan—51

Alexander, Corwin—13

APS (Anton Paul Sohn)—not indexed

Arlene (wife)—II, 1, 10, 12, 13, 19, 22, 39, 40, 42, 45, 63, 64, 67

Atcheson, James—86

B

Baker, Hinton—59, 62

Baker, Jim—20

Bolstad, Owen—48, 63, 64

Brady, Tom—III, 78, 79, 81, 82, 83, 84, 98

Brown, Harold—2, 3, 9

C

Cafferata, Treat—86

Callister, Jack—63

Cohen, Dave—25

Corning, Howard—1, 2, 3

Cudek, Ron—17, 22, 48

D

Daugherty, Bob—64

Day, Don—78

Donadio, Jim—13

E

Eric (son)—67

F

Farrell, Bruce—II, 47, 50

Father (Anton Peter Sohn)—II

Fulpert, Jim—44

Fulton, William—III

G

Ganchan, Richard—III, 85, 87, 88, 89, 90, 93, 98

Garib, Al—46, 47

Grayson, Jim—94, 95

H

Hedegard, Helen (mother-in-law)—67

Heumann, John—18, 21

Hope, Bob—83

Howard, Donald (cousin)—23, 38

Howard, Mabel (aunt)—23

Huffman, David—16, 19

Huxsoll, David—17, 71, 72

Hughes—84

I

Illig, Bill—14, 23, 44, 45, 47

J

Johnson, Charles—36

Johnson, President L.B.—II, IV

K

Katibah, Ed—15, 23, 45

King, Martin Luther—III

Knovick, George—10

Kristin (daughter)—67

L

Larson, Charles—II, 44, 63

Laubscher, Fred—45

Lucas, Dave—45

M

McNamara, Robert—21

Maehara, Ken—64

Mason, Dick—14, 25

Medawar, Mike—47

Mother (Ruth Marie Sohn)—II, III, 16, 19, 20

Myers, Warren—III, 17, 71, 72, 73, 74, 75, 77, 98

N

Nixon, Richard—V

Nitz, Gordon—78

P

Palmer, Arnold—10

Parks, Sam—64

Phil (Anton Phillip Sohn)— 1, 9, 10, 12, 39, 67, 70

R

Rieser, Al—10, 17, 18, 20, 22, 45

Ritzlin, Roger—64

Ropp, Bill—2, 3, 9

S

Salvadorini, V.A.—44, 48, 63

Sauls, Carl—78

Schieve, Don—63

Schrier, Bob—1, 3, 6, 7

Schwenk, Tom—64

Scichitand—84

Scully, Tom—1, 6

Sohn, Bill (William, brother)—39, 40, 44, 94, 95

T

Talsma, Jack—69

V

Vollrath, Victor—II

W

Walker, Bob (Louise's husband)—39

Walker, Louise (sister)—39

Weber, Amelia (aunt)—20, 40, 44

Wechsler—84

Weinstein, Phil—62

Westmoreland, General—21

I AM A "PROUD"
U.S. ARMY VETERAN

This book records forensic and anatomical pathology at the 9th Medical Laboratory in Saigon from April 1967 to April 1968 of the Vietnam War. I have also included photographs and information from 9th Medical Laboratory Veterinarian Captain Warren D. Myers, 7th Surgical Hospital Surgeon Captain Thomas W. Brady, and MACV-SOG Navy Physician Lieutenant Richard P. Ganchan.

The 9th Medical Laboratory did all autopsies and surgical pathology cases for U.S. Forces. The most common autopsy (over 40%) was the result of a helicopter accident that flew at top-speed at tree-top level to avoid enemy fire. Most of the remaining demonstrate the stress of combat with suicides, murders, fake injuries, and accidents.

Unfortunately, I did not keep pathology practice notes and photographs since they were sent to the Armed Forces Institute of Pathology (AFIP) in Washington, D.C. This book is written from my personal notes, letters, and photographs.

This is the only book written about pathology and veterinarian medicine during the Vietnam War. However, it is not the first book about medicine in the Vietnam war. In 2017, my Indiana University School of Medicine classmate, Nephrologist Captain James Donadio, Jr. published an excellent book, *From Mayo Clinic to Vietnam: Memoirs of a Physician Serving in the War*.